FRANCESCO CICCOLELLA

BETWEEN THE LINES

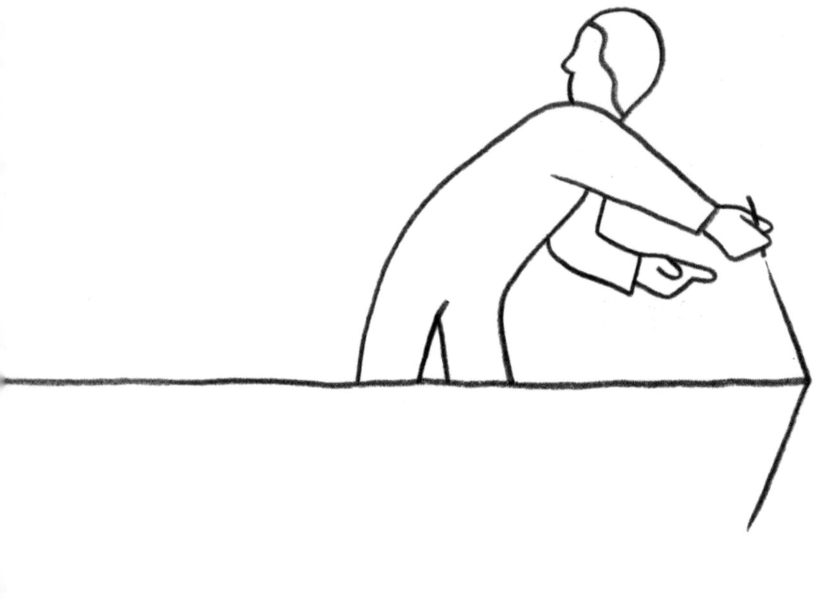

Verlag für moderne Kunst

ABOUT A DECADE AGO, ON AN ORDINARY WEEKDAY MORNING THAT REMAINS BLURRY AND FRAGMENTED IN MY MIND, THE COURSE OF MY LIFE TOOK AN UNEXPECTED TURN.

I WAS IN MY EARLY TWENTIES, STUDYING AT ART SCHOOL IN VIENNA, WHEN MY MOM'S WEEKLY CALL CAME IN AT AN UNUSUAL TIME.

AS I ANSWERED, WORDS FAILED ME AND, WITHIN ITS BREVITY, THAT CALL SEEMED TO LAST FOR WHAT FELT LIKE AN ETERNITY.

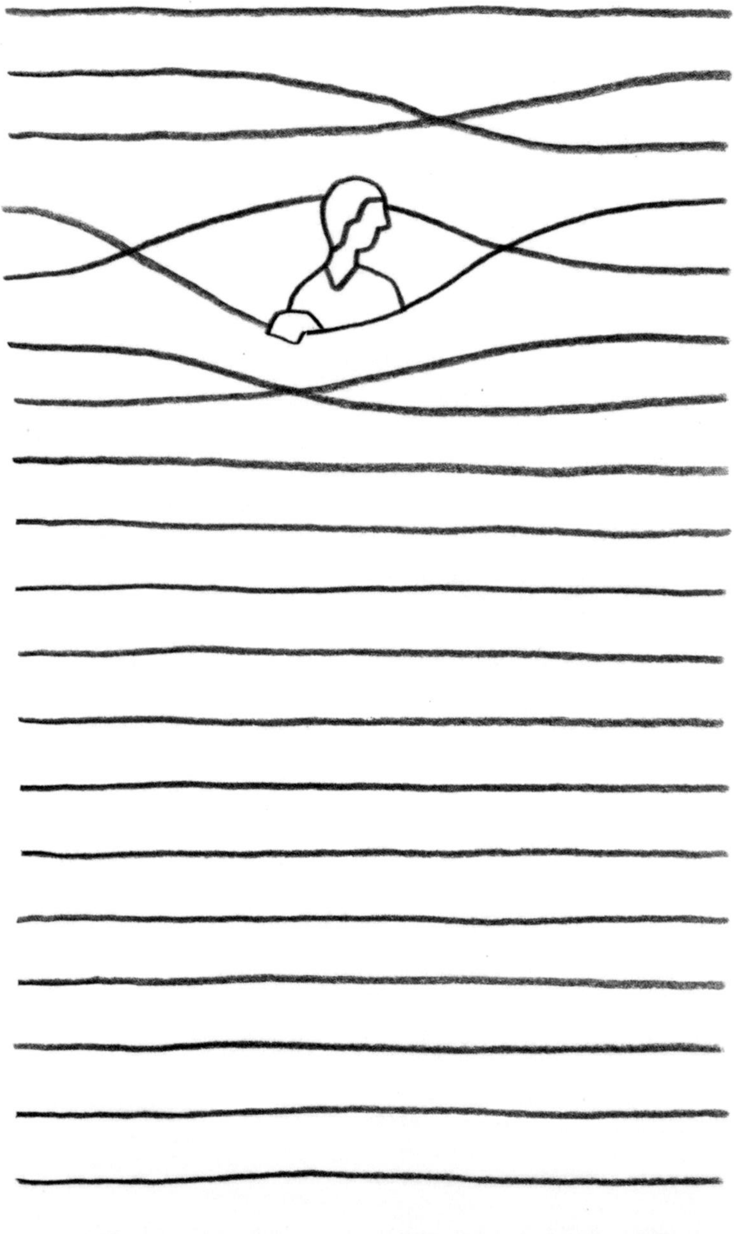

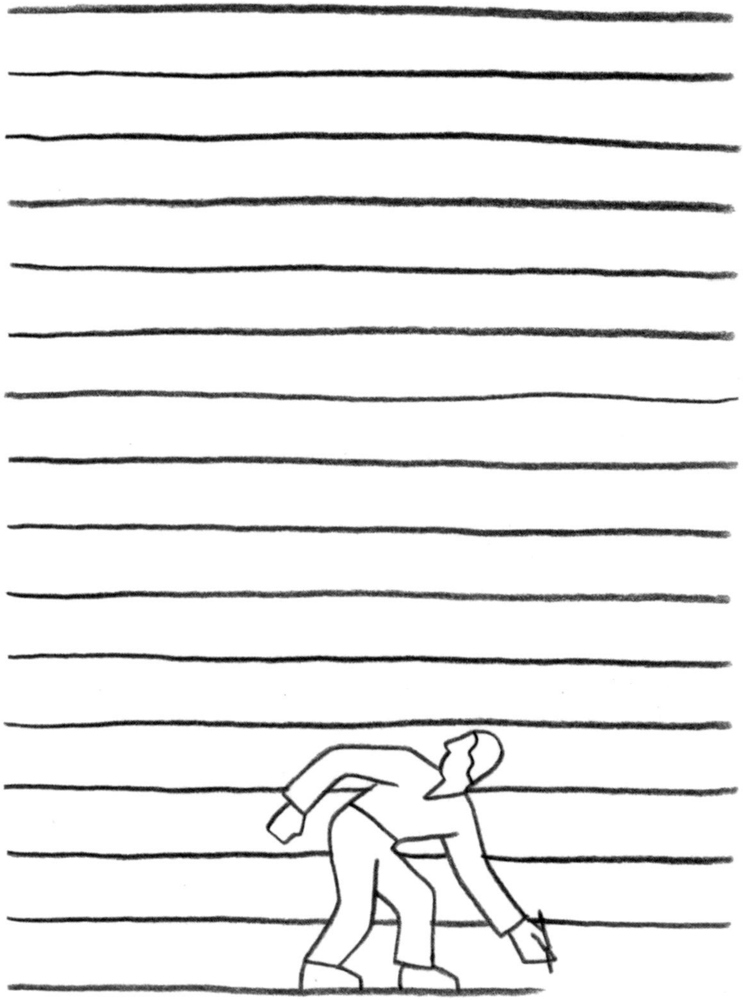

IN THE GRIP OF WHAT TURNED OUT TO BE SEVERE DEPRESSION, MY BROTHER HAD MADE A DESPERATE ATTEMPT TO TAKE HIS OWN LIFE.

HE SURVIVED, BUT IT LEFT ITS MARK, BRINGING PRACTICAL CHANGES AND NEW CHALLENGES TO HIS DAILY LIFE.

THE IMPACT WAS PROFOUND, NOT JUST ON HIM BUT ALSO ON THOSE CLOSE TO HIM.

FROM ONE DAY TO THE NEXT, OUR LITTLE FAMILY OF FOUR FOUND ITSELF WEATHERING THE OVERWHELMING CHAOS OF AN UNANNOUNCED STORM.

PROGRESS AND FURTHER SETBACKS ALTERNATED ON A WEEKLY, SOMETIMES DAILY, BASIS, TESTING OUR RESILIENCE AND FAMILY BONDS.

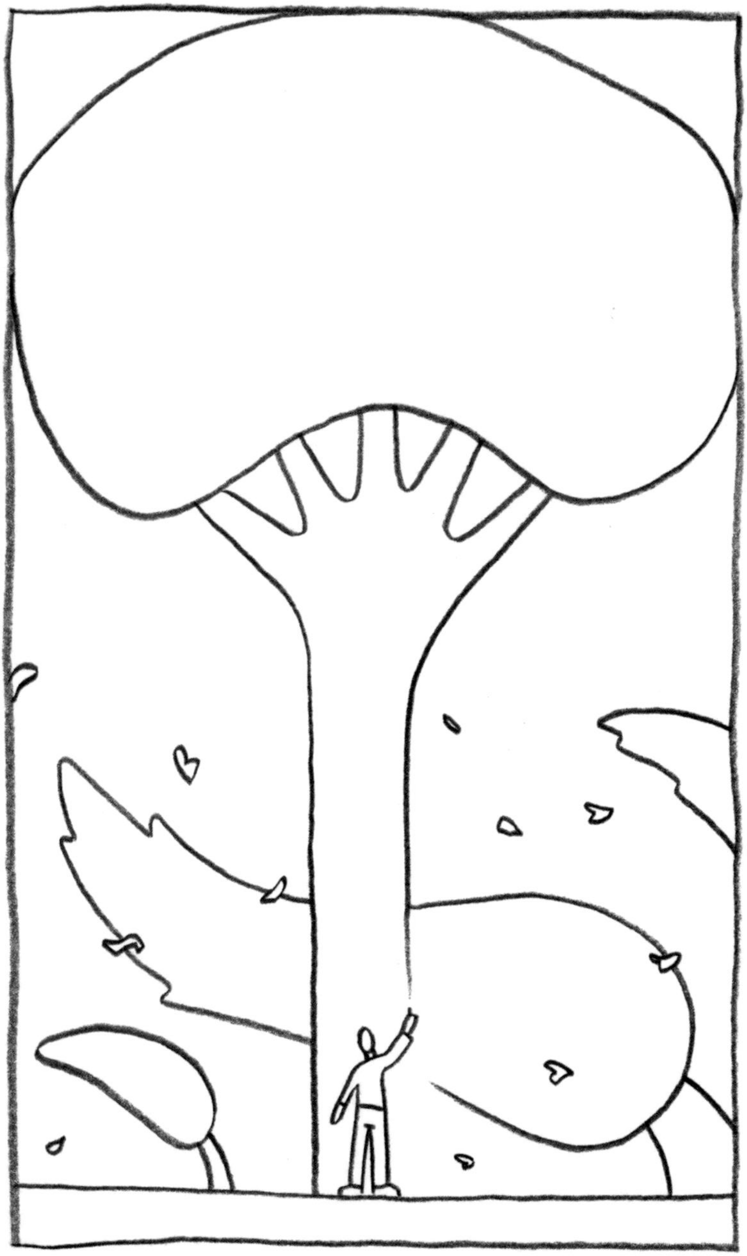

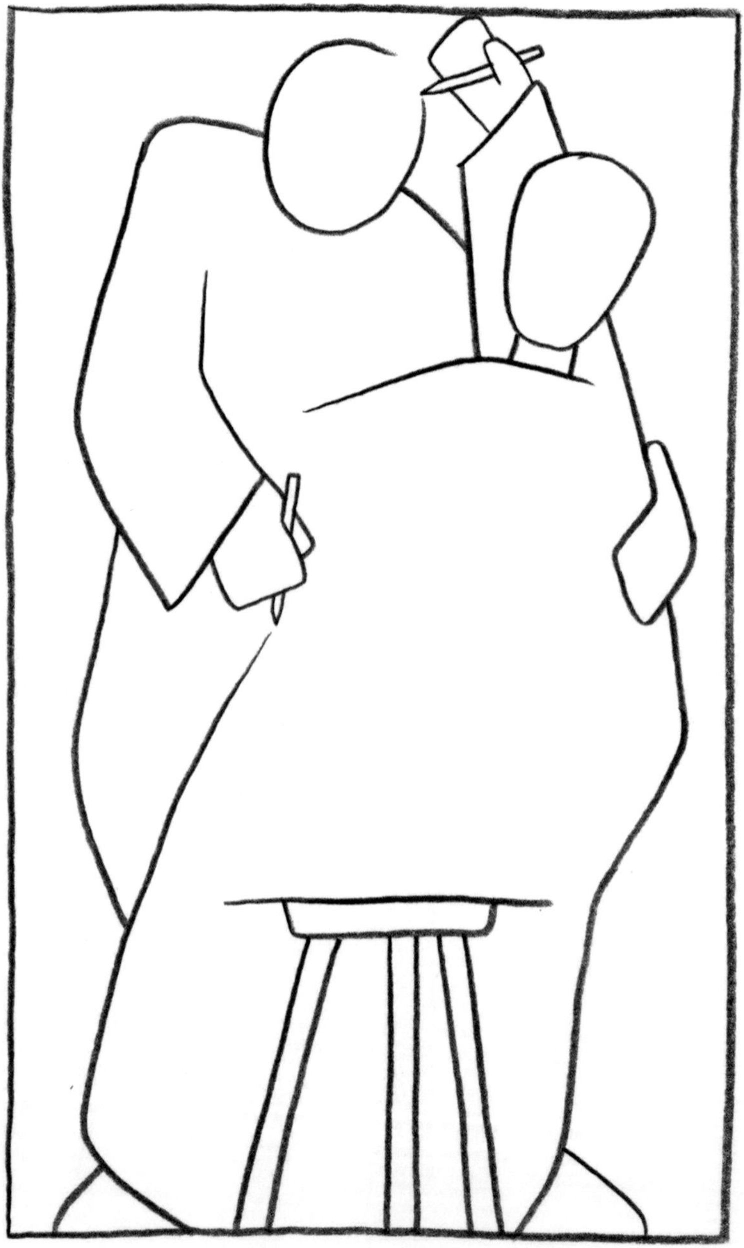

MY BROTHER IS TWO YEARS YOUNGER THAN ME.

TWO YEARS THAT, SINCE WE WERE LITTLE, HE EASILY MADE UP FOR WITH HIS GROWN-UP MANNER AND KEEN SENSE OF HUMOR.

WE WERE CLOSE, NOT JUST IN AGE, BUT IN EVERY ASPECT OF OUR LIVES.

WE SHARED THE SAME CHILDHOOD FRIENDS, TRAVELED AROUND EUROPE, AND PLAYED IN THE SAME MEDIOCRE TEENAGE BAND.

WHILE WE SPOKE GERMAN WITH OUR MOM AND ITALIAN WITH OUR DAD, MY BROTHER AND I OFTEN UNDERSTOOD EACH OTHER WITHOUT WORDS.

AND STILL, I NEVER SAW THIS COMING.

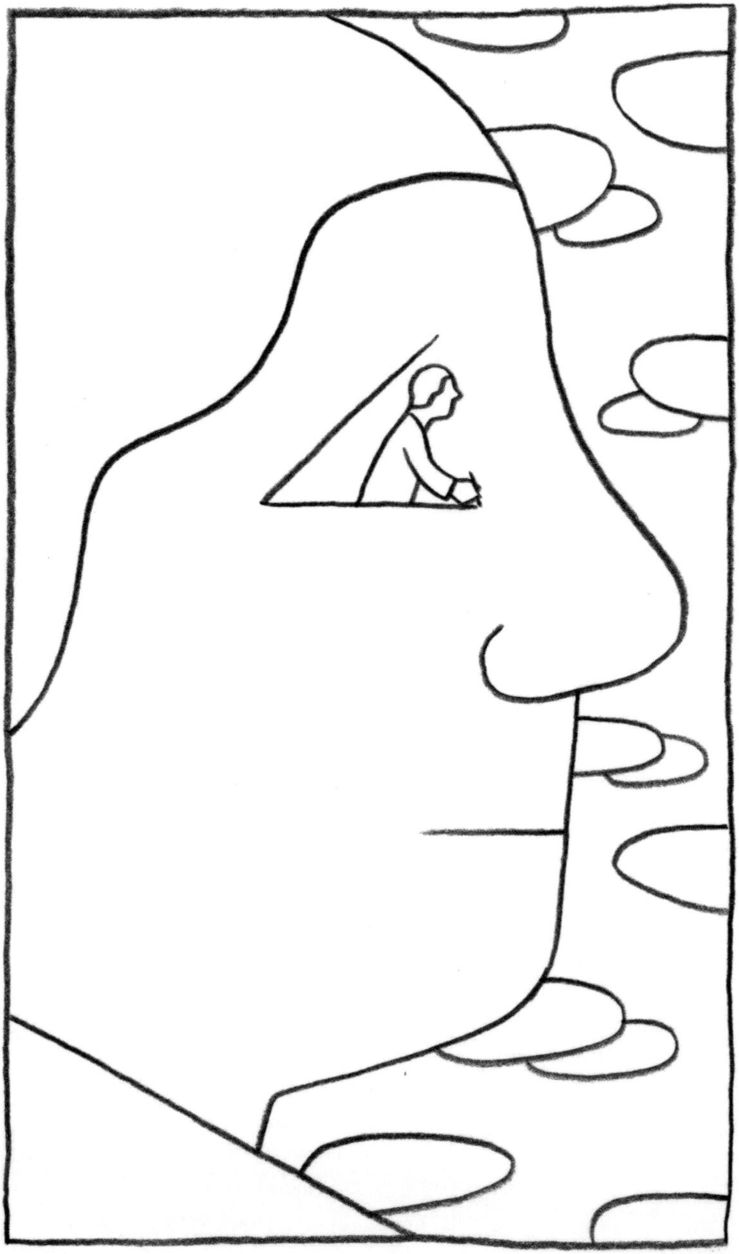

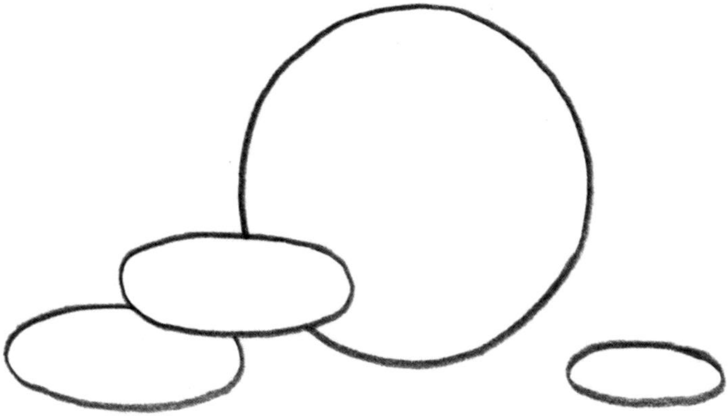

ONLY NOW, THE DENSE FOG THAT ENVELOPED HIM BECAME GLARINGLY OBVIOUS - THE KIND THAT DISTORTS REALITY, TRAPS THE MIND IN DESPAIR, AND RENDERS YOU SEEMINGLY HELPLESS.

YET, EVERY TIME I TRIED TO GRASP IT, IT SLIPPED THROUGH MY FINGERS.

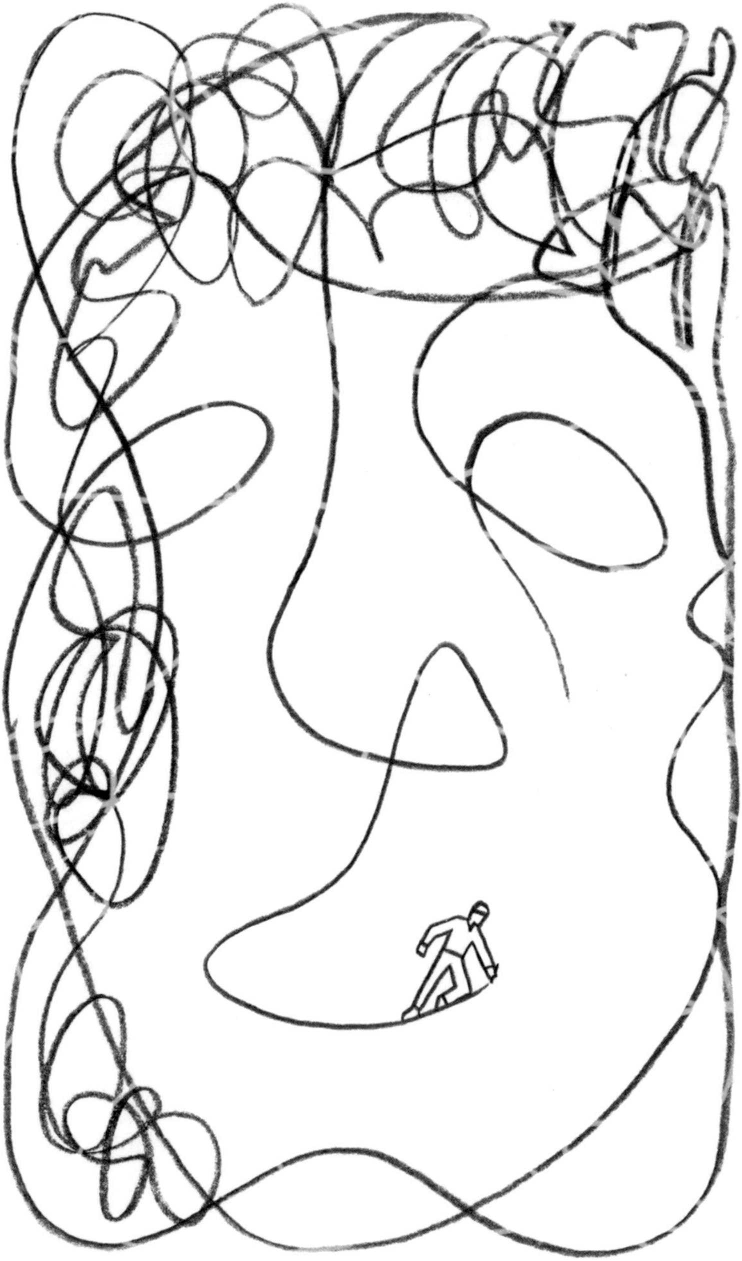

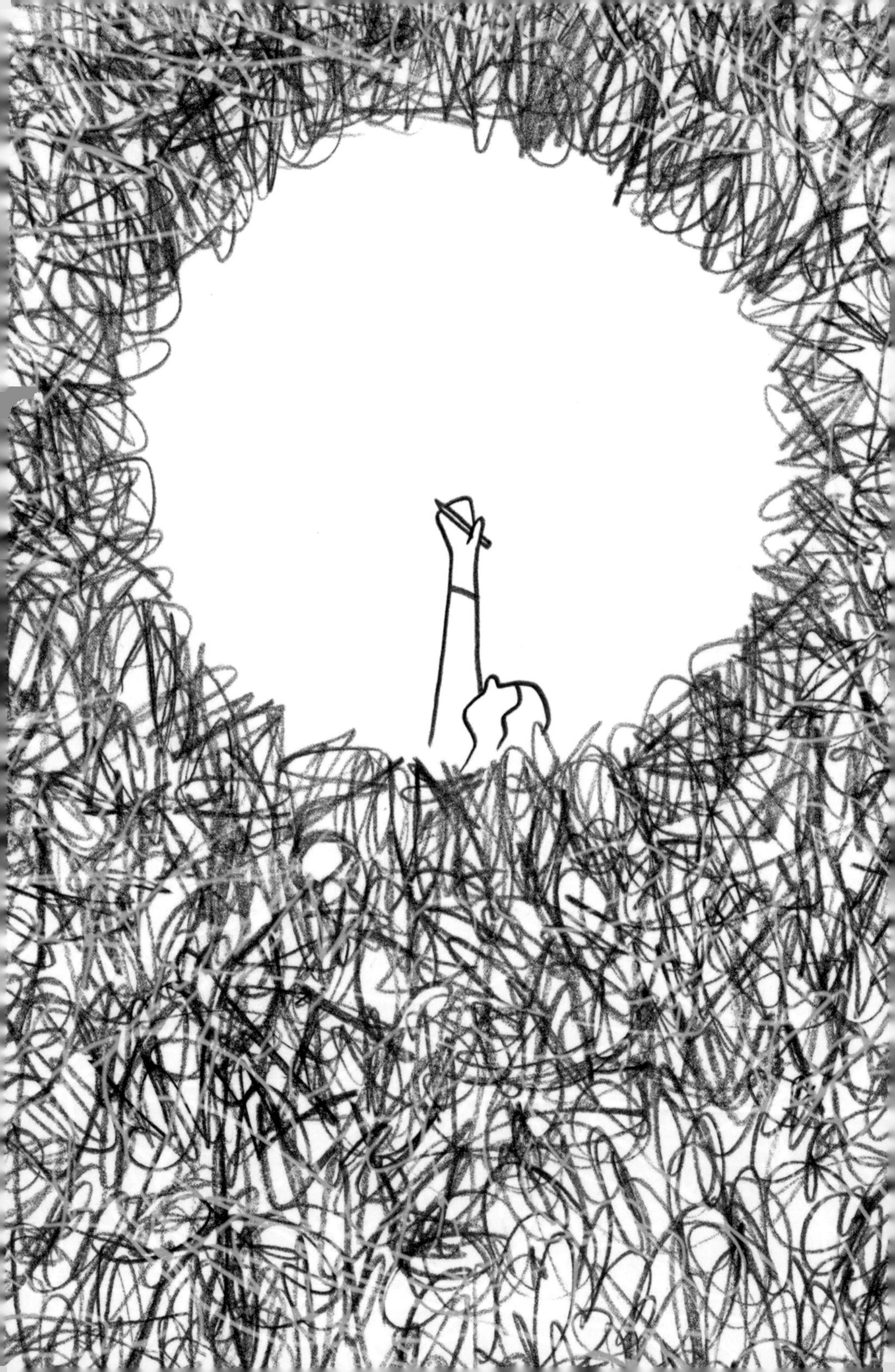

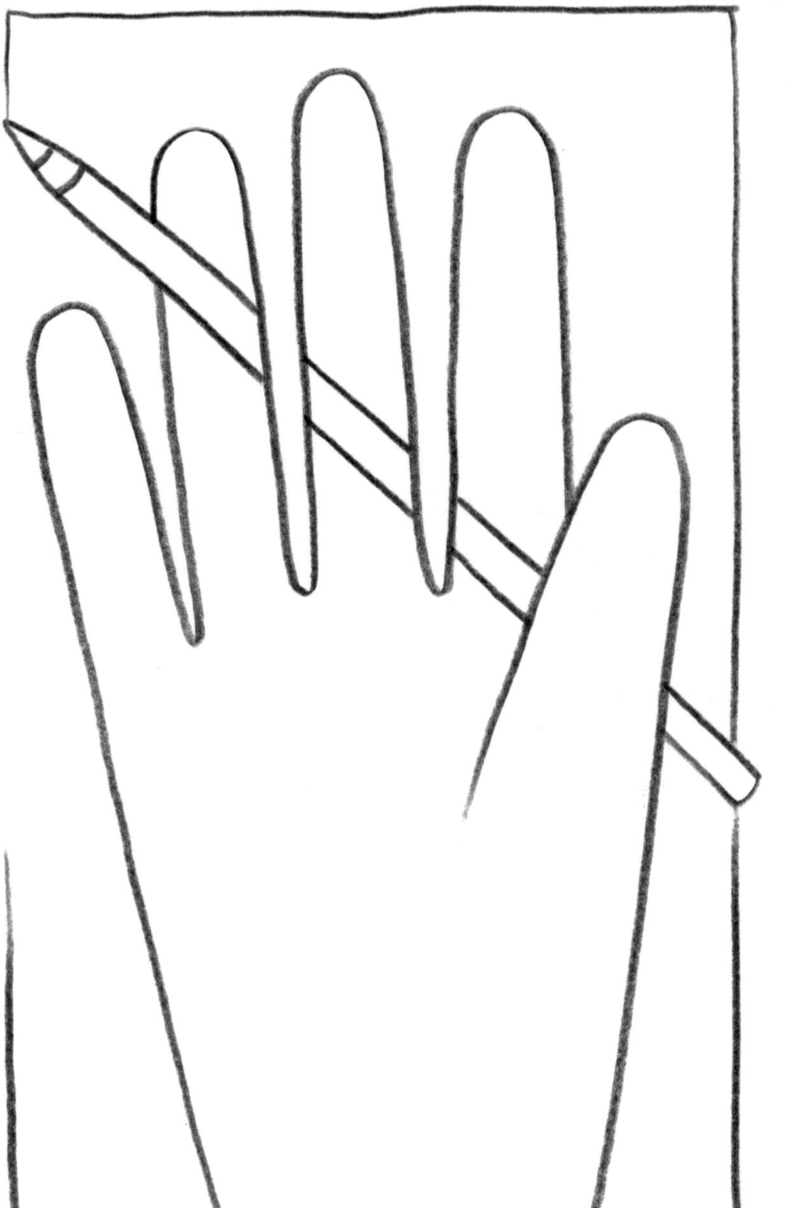

I DID MY BEST TO SUPPORT MY BROTHER ON HIS LONG AND TIRING PATH TO RECOVERY.

OVER THE YEARS, I HAVE LEARNED THAT JUST BEING THERE AND LISTENING CAN SOMETIMES BE MORE VALUABLE THAN TRYING TO SOLVE ANOTHER PERSON'S PROBLEMS.

THE PAST DECADE HAS BEEN BOTH AN INSIGHTFUL AND EXHAUSTING EDUCATION IN EMPATHY, COMPASSION, AND PATIENCE.

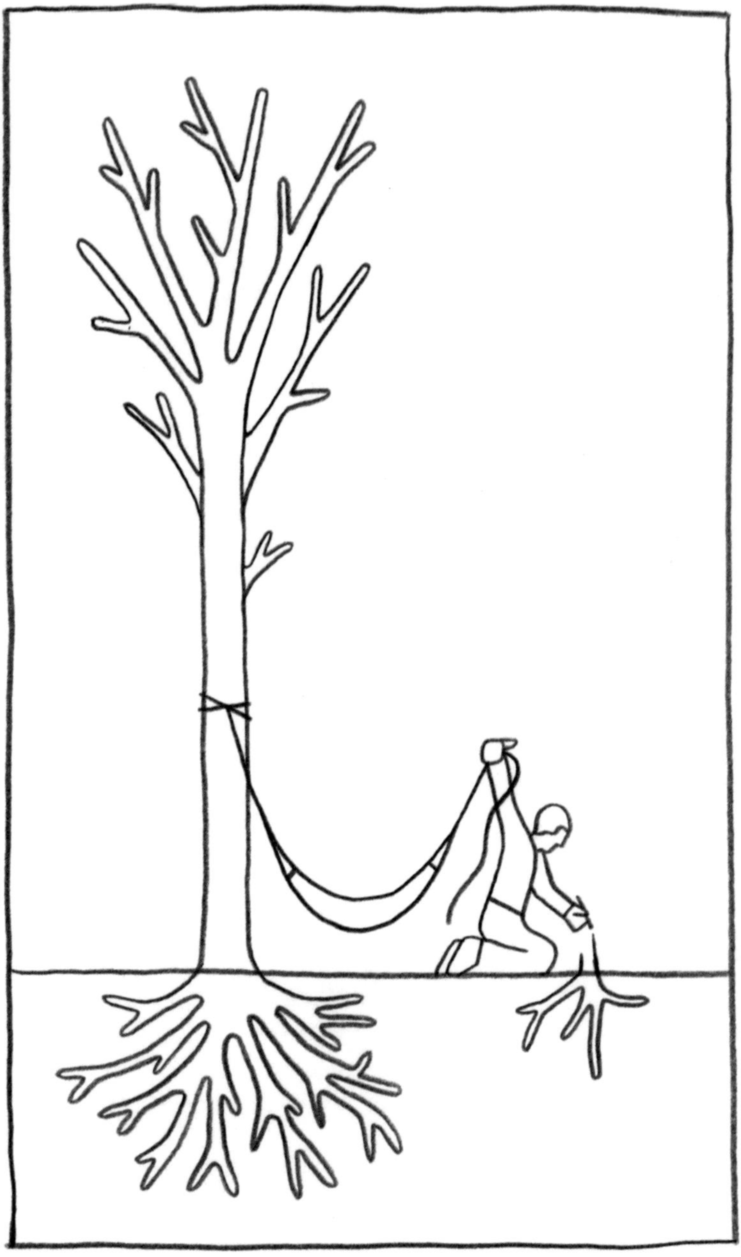

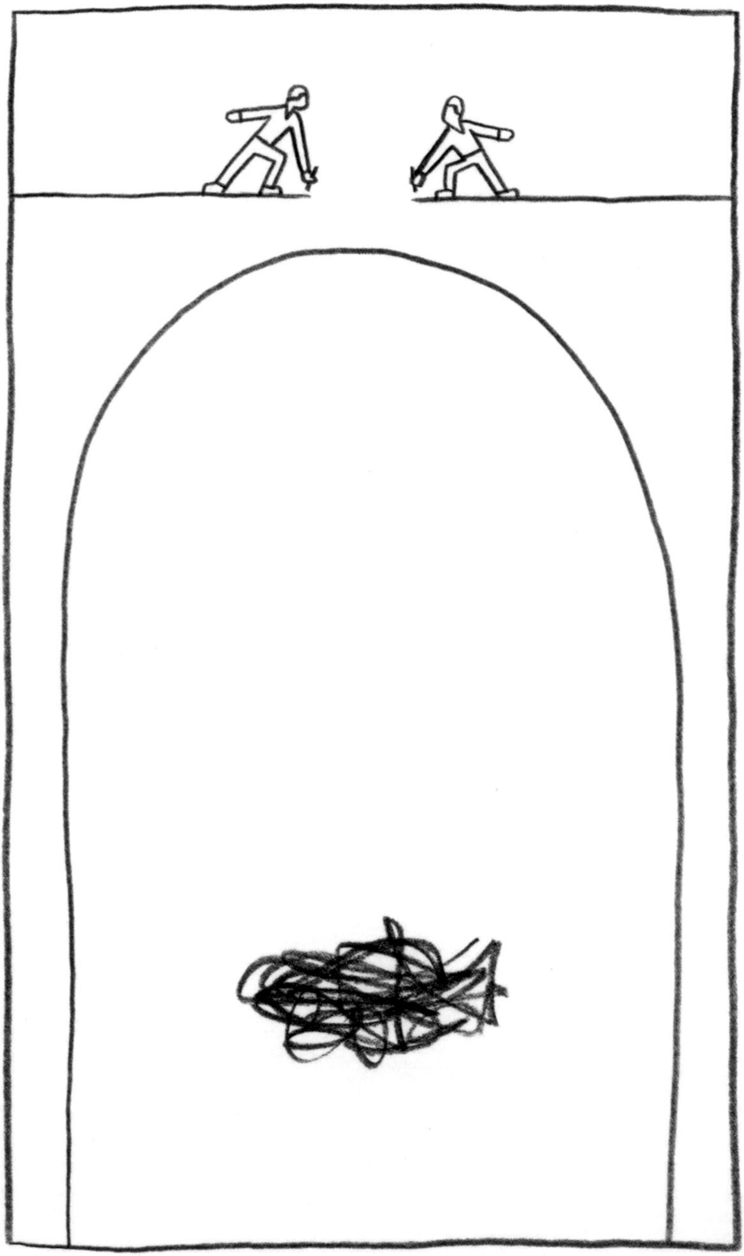

AT TIMES,
I HAD TO KEEP A HEALTHY DISTANCE.

SINCE HIS ATTEMPT,
MY BROTHER AND I WENT THROUGH PERIODS OF ESTRANGEMENT WITH LITTLE TO NO CONTACT, FOLLOWED BY EMOTIONAL MOMENTS OF RECONNECTION.

SOMETIMES HIS INVISIBLE COMPANION
WAS IN THE ROOM WITH US. SOMETIMES HE WASN'T.

EACH TIME I TRAVELED FROM VIENNA TO OUR HOMETOWN OF SALZBURG TO VISIT HIM, THE FOG GREETED ME WITH VARYING DEGREES OF THICKNESS.

Fig. ❶
BOB DYLAN
BOOTS OF SPANISH LEATHER

Fig. ❷
THE TALLEST MAN ON EARTH
I'M A STRANGER NOW

Fig. ❸
STEAMING SATELLITES
HOW DARE YOU!

THERE WERE MOMENTS WHEN IT SEEMED AS IF IT HAD LIFTED, FUELING MY HOPES THAT ONE DAY IT COULD VANISH ENTIRELY.

Fig. ❹
DAVID RAMIREZ
TIME

Fig. ❺
PIERANGELO BERTOLI
EPPURE SOFFIA

Fig. ❻
LUCY DACUS
DANCING IN THE DARK

A GOOD INDICATOR OF MY BROTHER'S CURRENT MOOD WAS THE MUSIC THAT ECHOED THROUGH OUR PARENTS' HOUSE VIA THE BLUETOOTH SPEAKERS IN HIS ROOM.

Fig. ❼
LCD SOUNDSYSTEM
ALL MY FRIENDS

Fig. ❽
MUMFORD & SONS
AWAKE MY SOUL

Fig. ❾
LUCIO BATTISTI
CON IL NASTRO ROSA

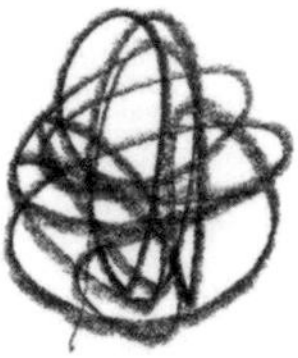

Fig. ❶

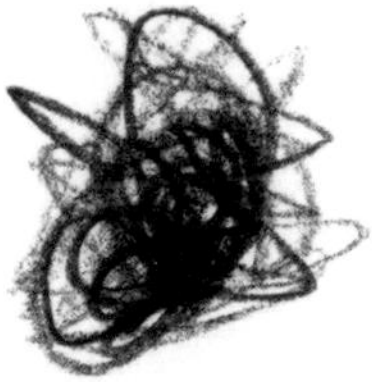

Fig. ❷

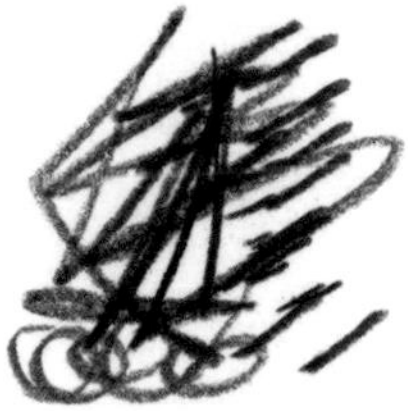

Fig. ❸

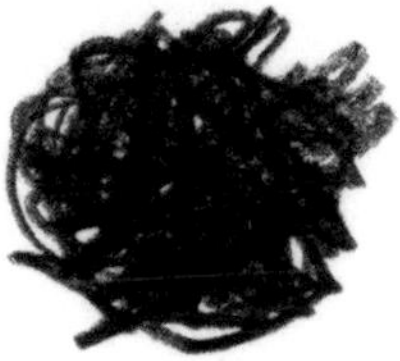

Fig. ❹

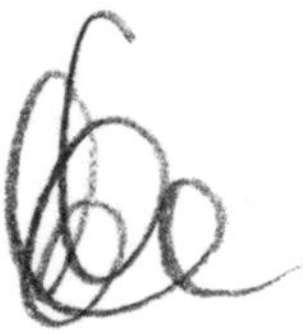

Fig. ❺

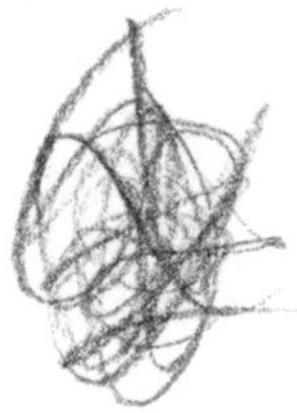

Fig. ❻

Fig. ❼

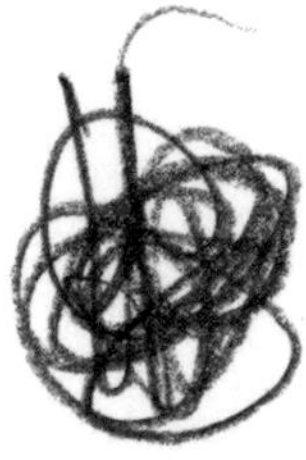

Fig. ❽

Fig. ❾

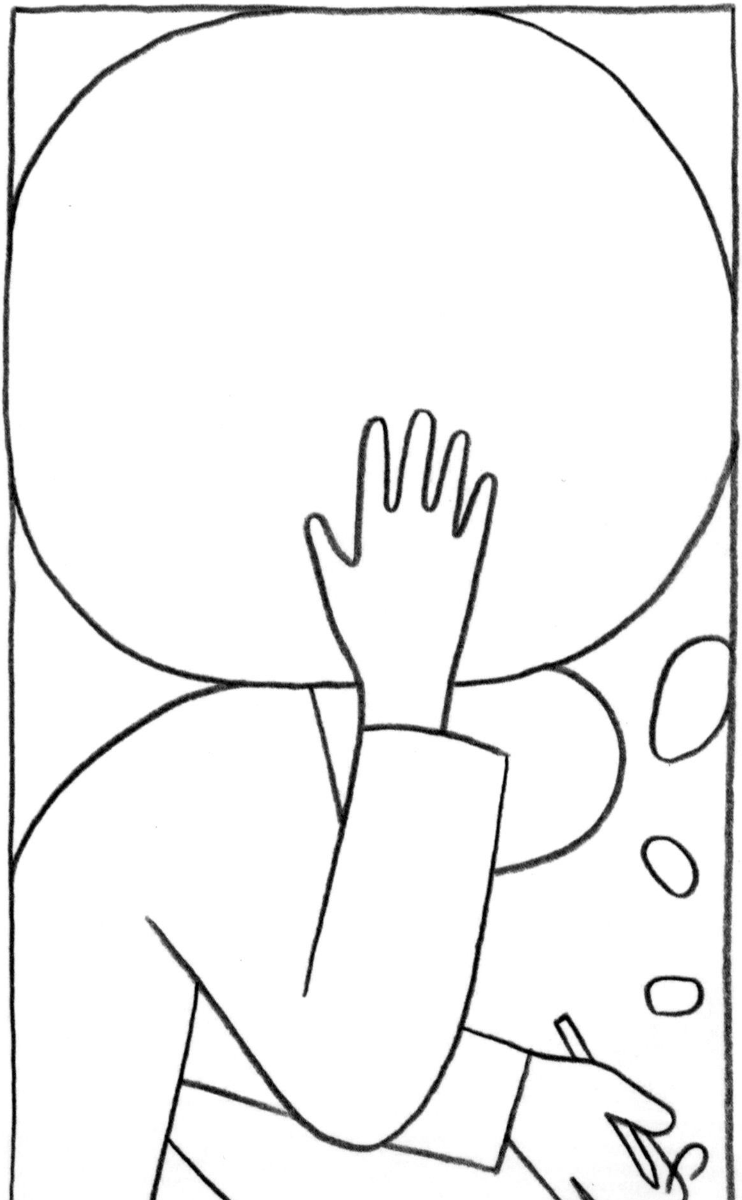

I, TOO, STRUGGLED.

SEEING SUCH PAIN AND SADNESS IN HIM WITHOUT THE POWER TO ALLEVIATE IT WAS AGONIZING, IF NOT UNBEARABLE.

I FELT ALL SORTS OF FEELINGS AND, AT TIMES, NEGLECTED MY OWN WELL-BEING.

THE FLURRY OF EMOTIONS
INCLUDED:

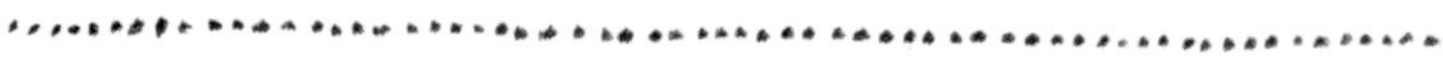

Grief

Sadness

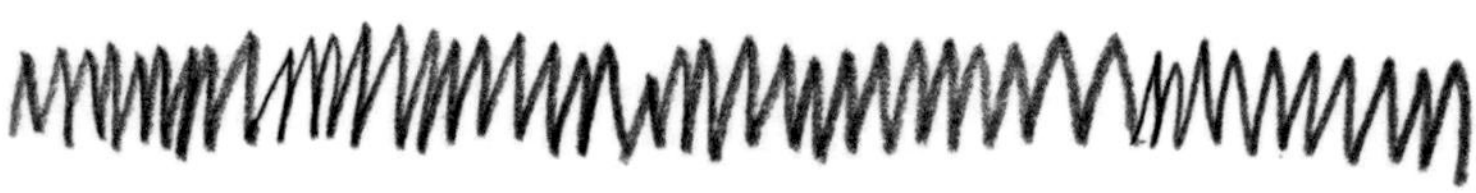

Anger

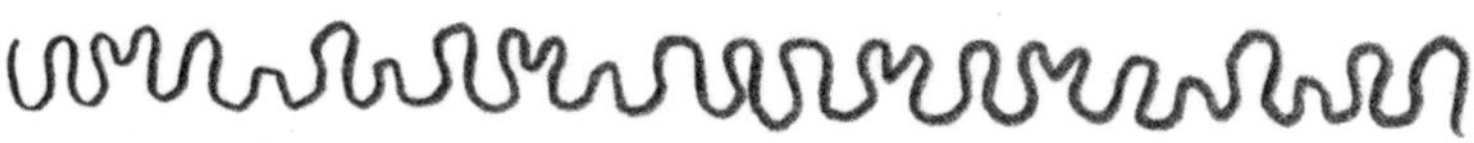

Helplessness

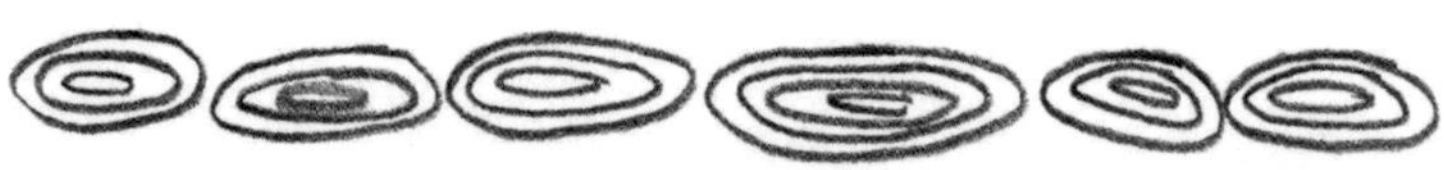

Frustration

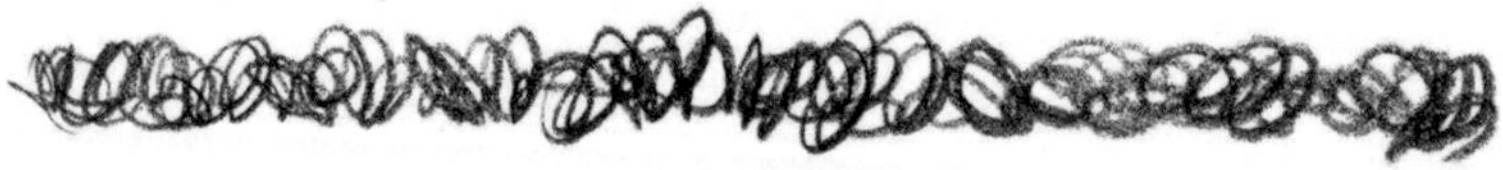

Embarrassment

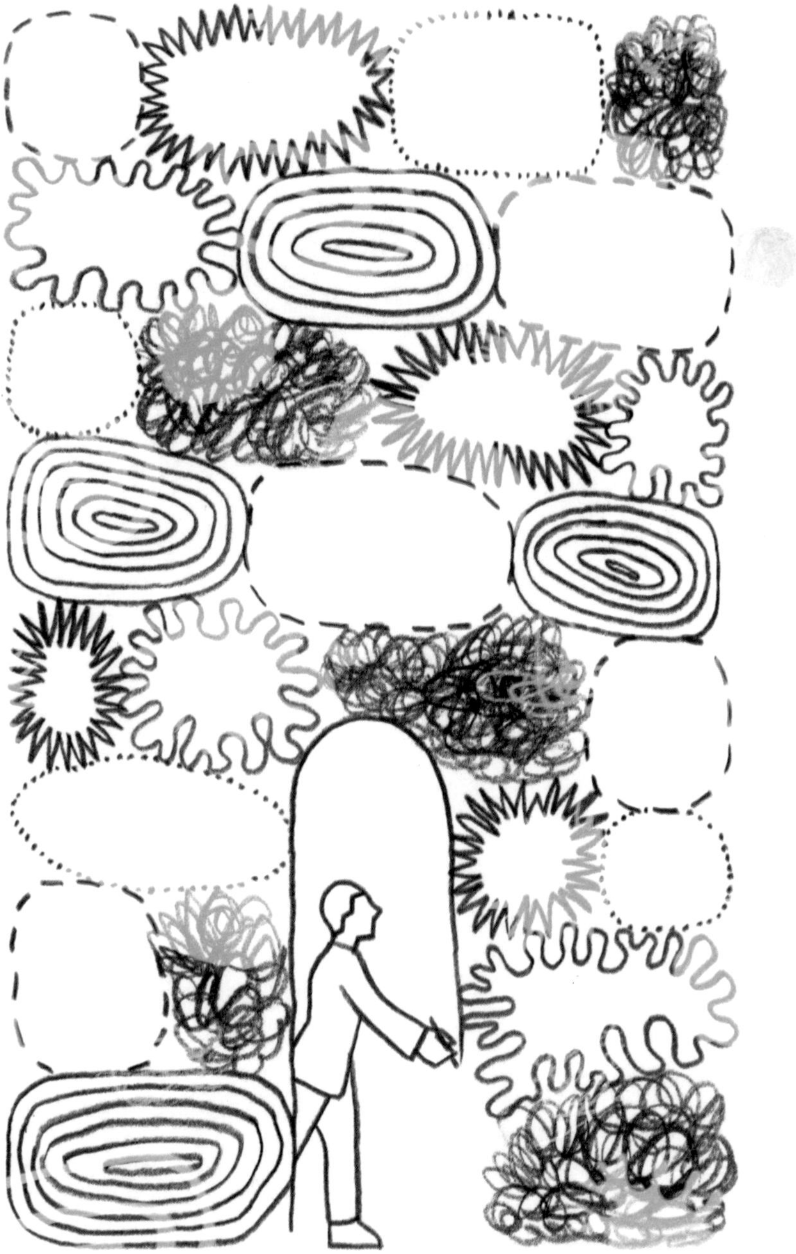

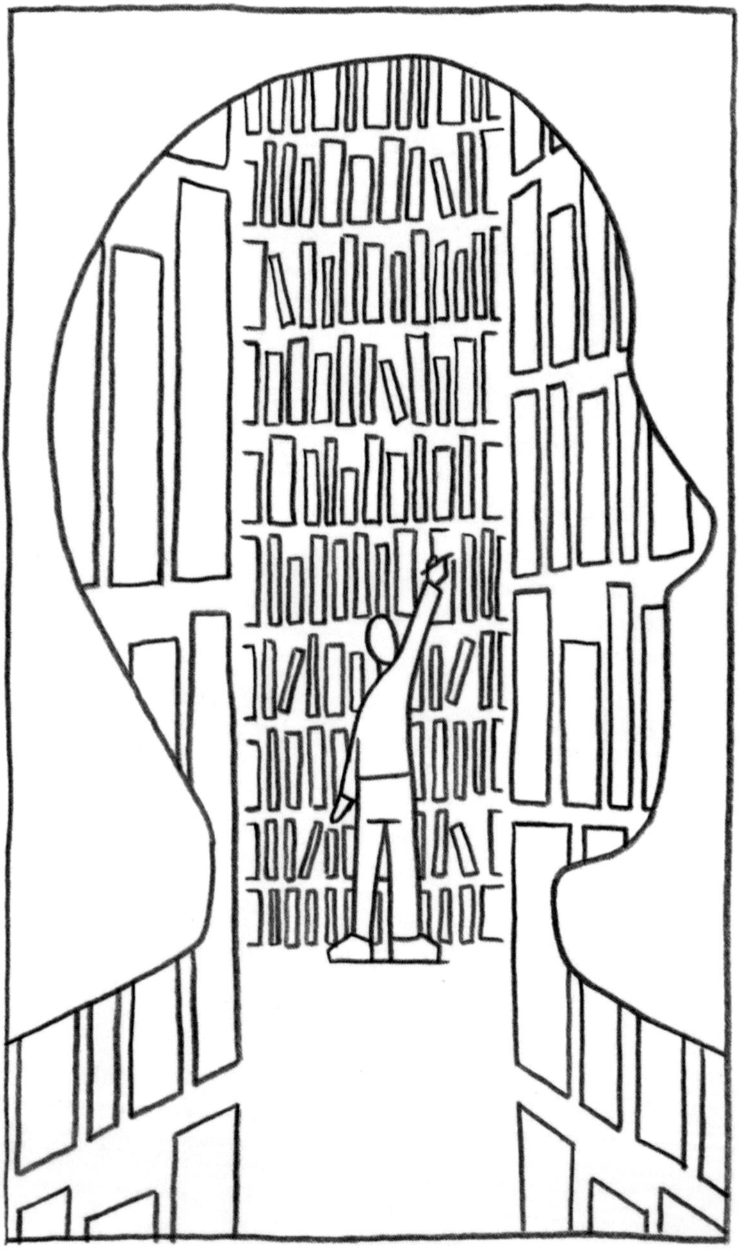

I SOUGHT SOLACE IN TRYING TO GAIN A DEEPER UNDERSTANDING OF MY BROTHER'S MENTAL ILLNESS.

I YEARNED TO MAKE SENSE OF IT.

ALONG THE WAY, I STUMBLED UPON A THEORY KNOWN AS THE "*HEDONIC TREADMILL,*" DEVELOPED BY PSYCHOLOGISTS PHILIP BRICKMAN AND DONALD CAMPBELL.

IT SUGGESTS THAT, REGARDLESS OF TEMPORARY UPS OR DOWNS IN LIFE, WE ALL HAVE A TENDENCY TO REVERT TO OUR INDIVIDUAL BASELINE LEVEL OF HAPPINESS.

AT SOME POINT, I BEGAN TO NOTICE A CORRELATION IN OUR EMOTIONAL STATES.

OFTENTIMES, OUR UPS AND DOWNS, IT SEEMED, WERE MOVING IN TANDEM.

WHENEVER HE WAS DOING WELL AND FEELING GOOD, I WAS TOO, AND VICE VERSA.

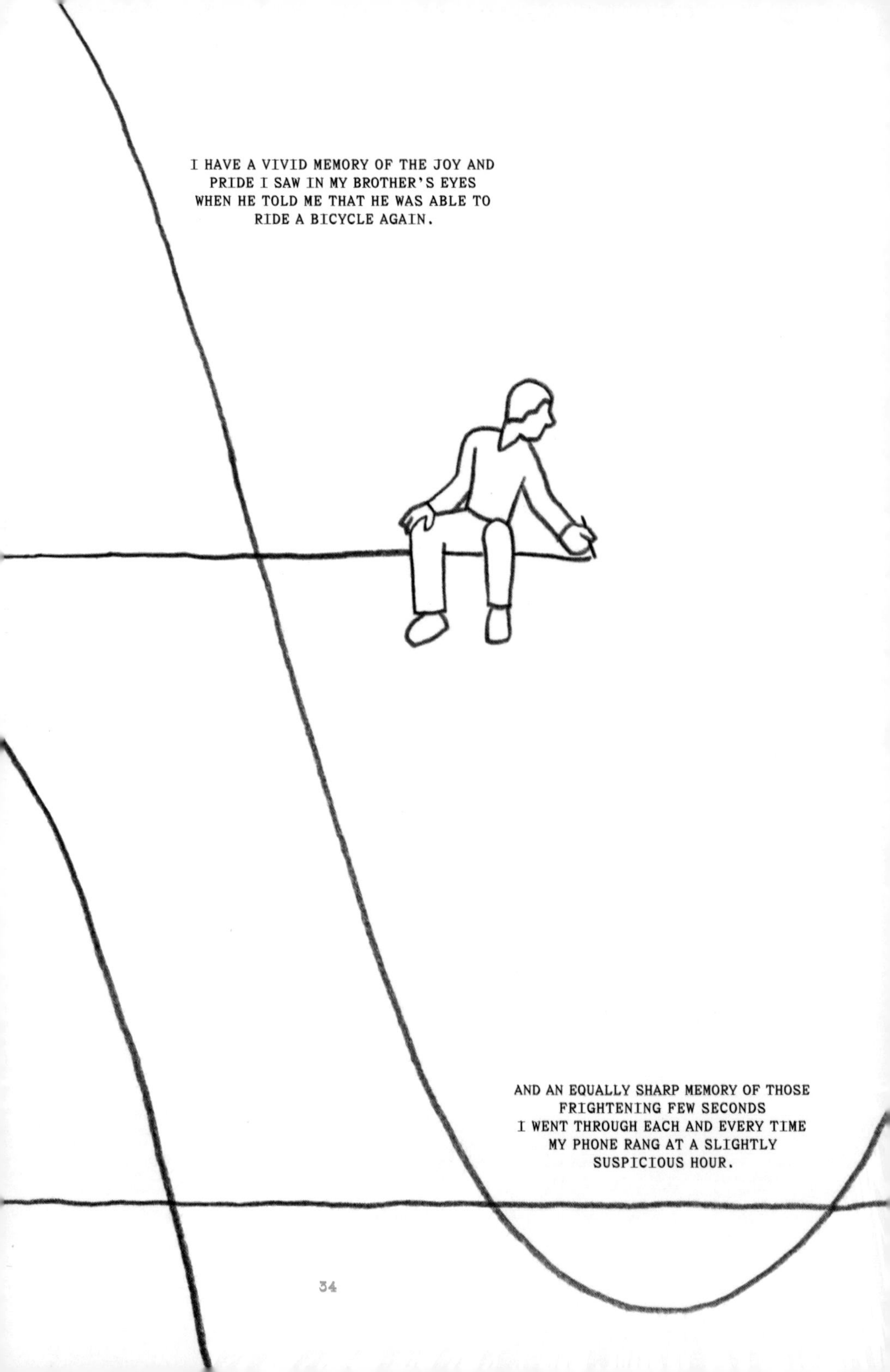
I HAVE A VIVID MEMORY OF THE JOY AND PRIDE I SAW IN MY BROTHER'S EYES WHEN HE TOLD ME THAT HE WAS ABLE TO RIDE A BICYCLE AGAIN.
AND AN EQUALLY SHARP MEMORY OF THOSE FRIGHTENING FEW SECONDS I WENT THROUGH EACH AND EVERY TIME MY PHONE RANG AT A SLIGHTLY SUSPICIOUS HOUR.

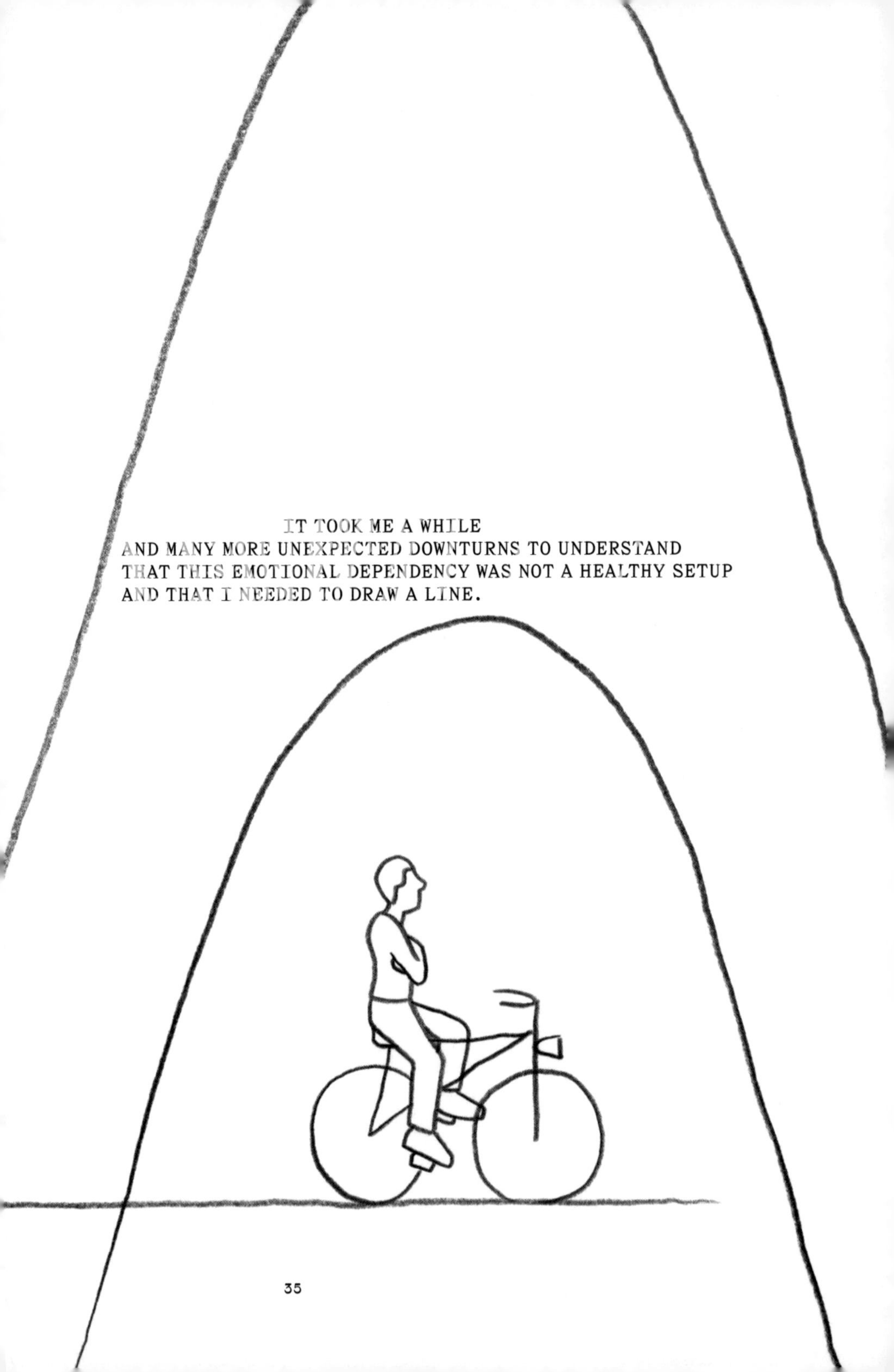
IT TOOK ME A WHILE
AND MANY MORE UNEXPECTED DOWNTURNS TO UNDERSTAND
THAT THIS EMOTIONAL DEPENDENCY WAS NOT A HEALTHY SETUP
AND THAT I NEEDED TO DRAW A LINE.

36

A THERAPIST SUGGESTED THAT IT MIGHT BE PRESUMPTUOUS TO THINK THAT ONE COULD FULLY COMPREHEND MY BROTHER'S CONDITION.

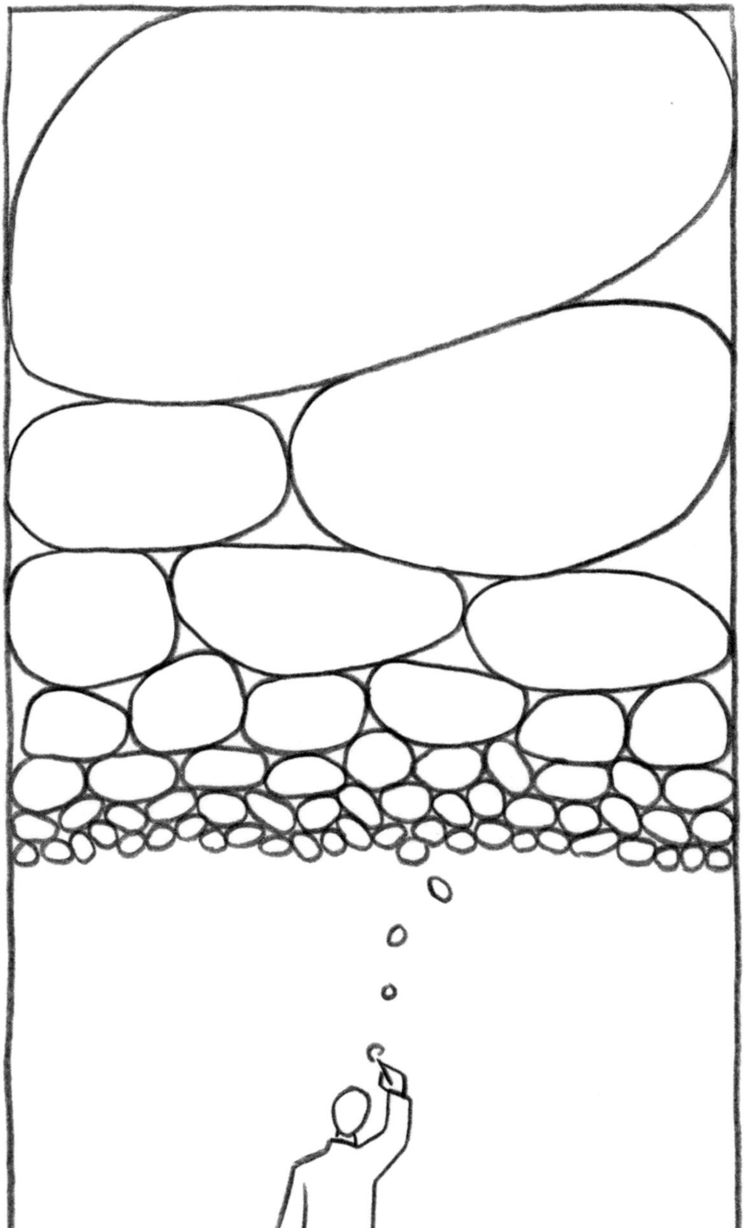

I AGREED
BUT KEPT TRYING.

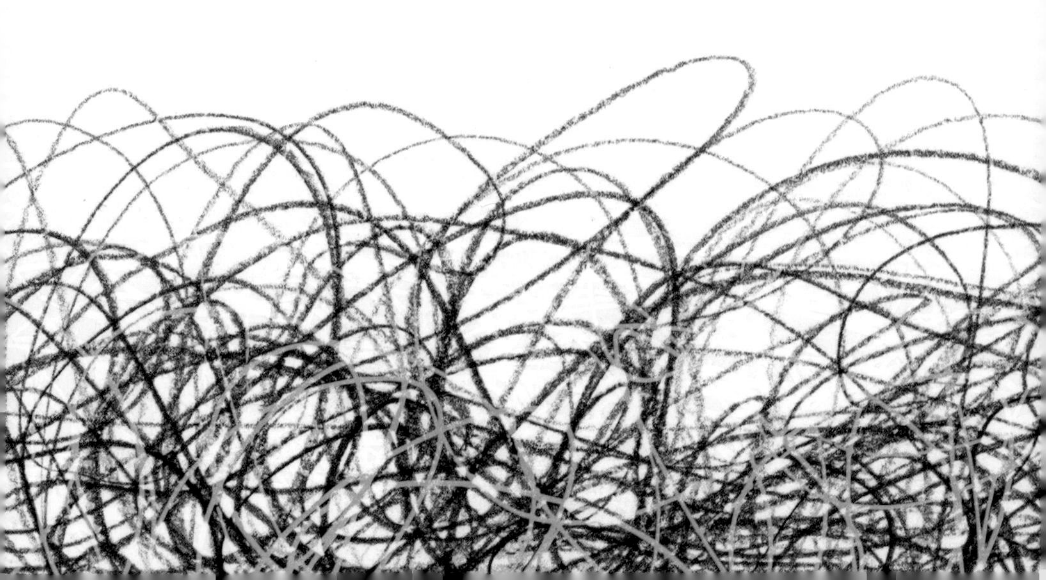

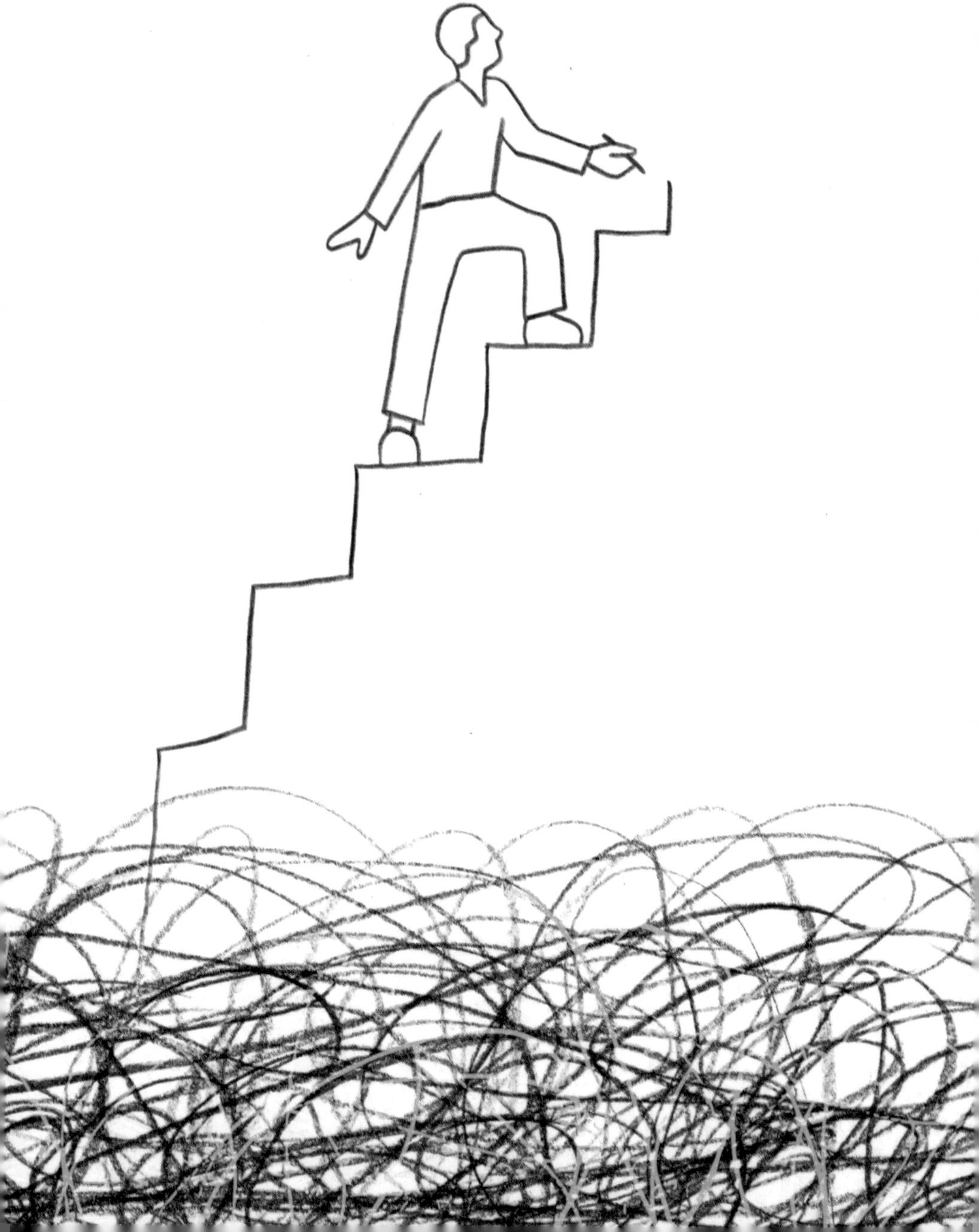

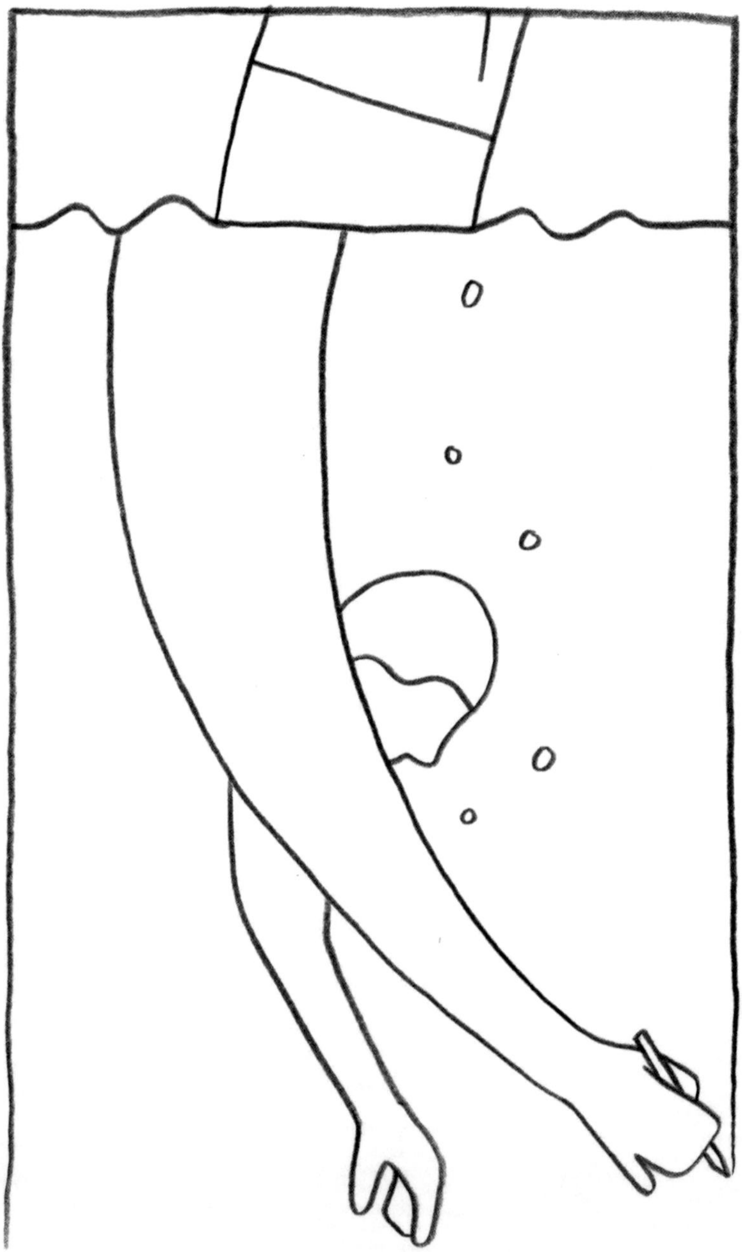

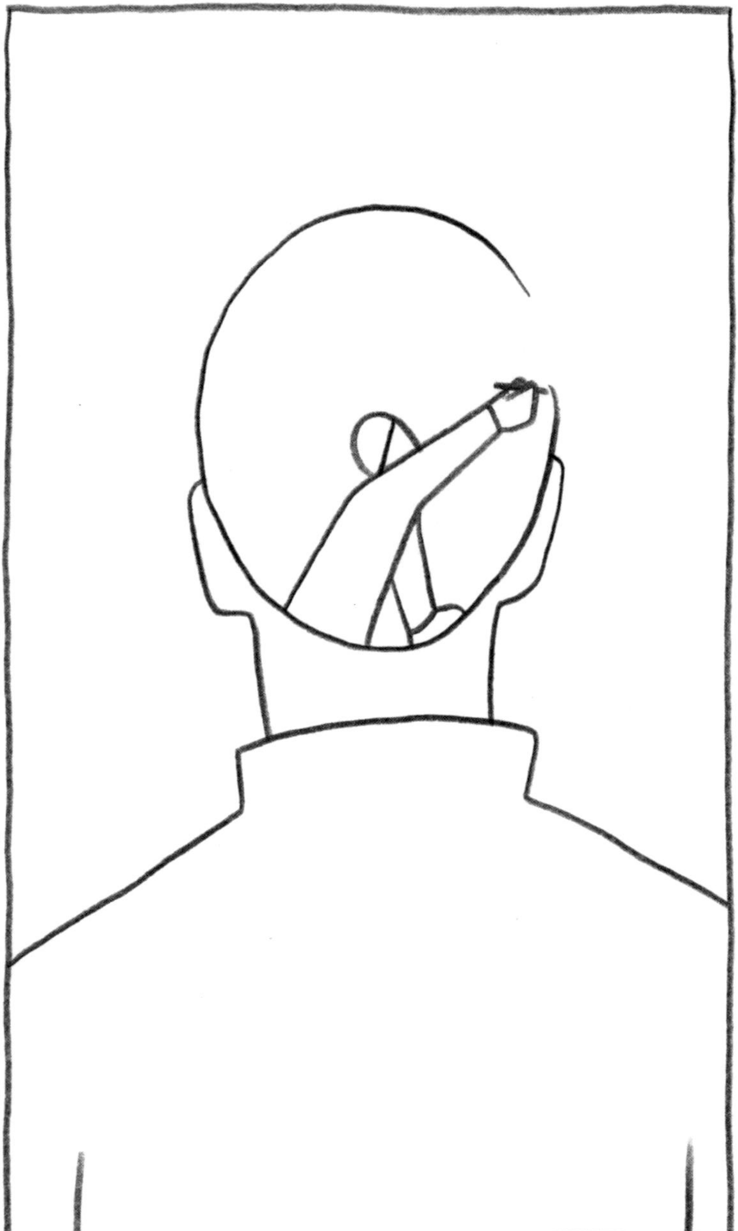

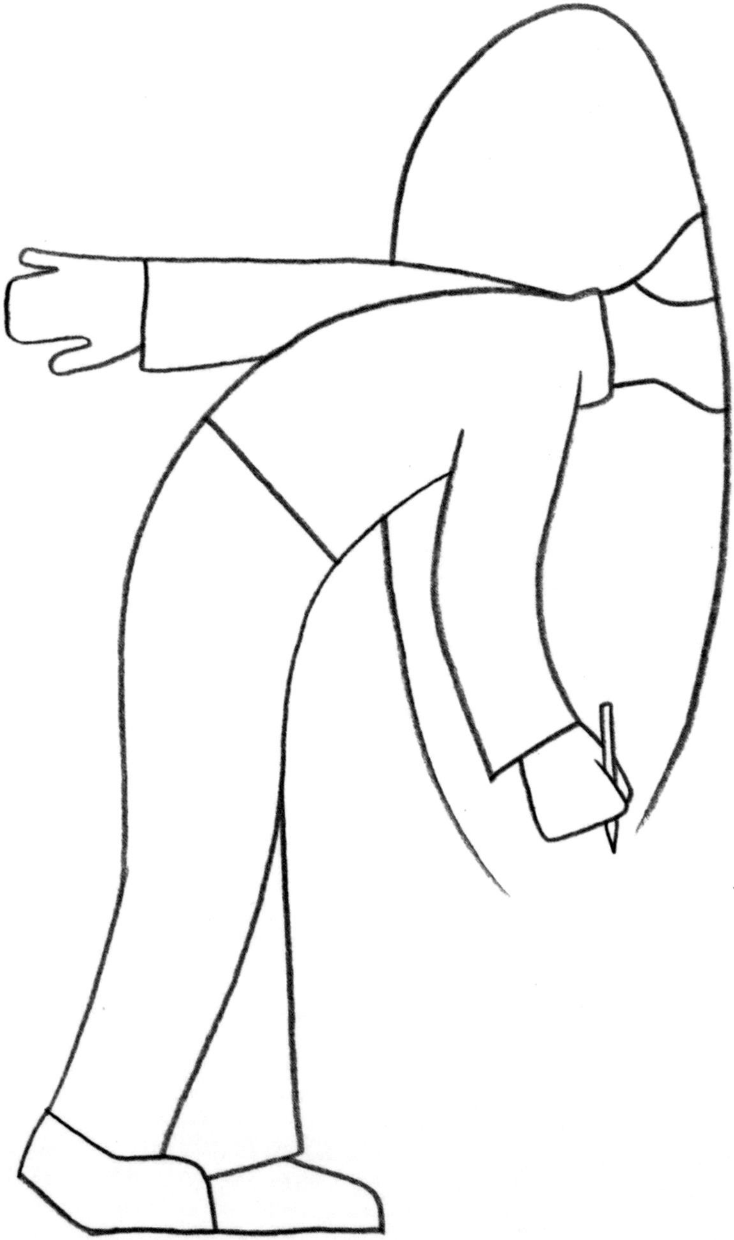

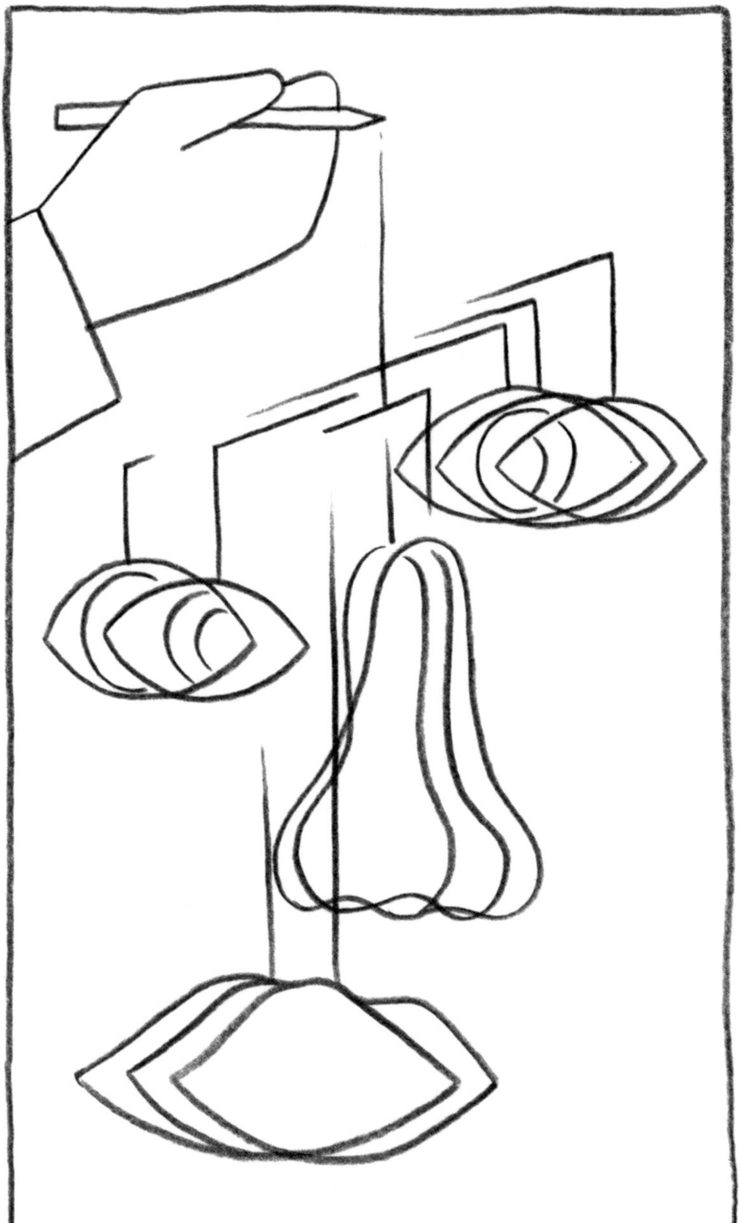

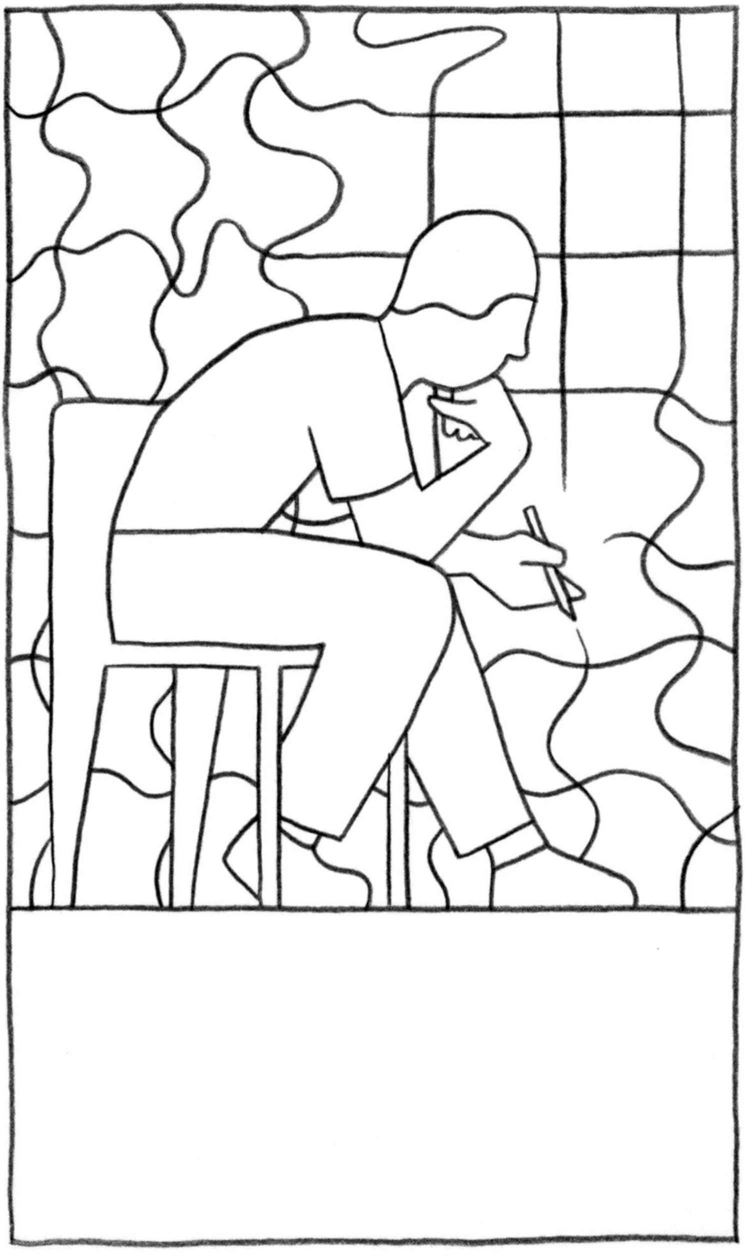

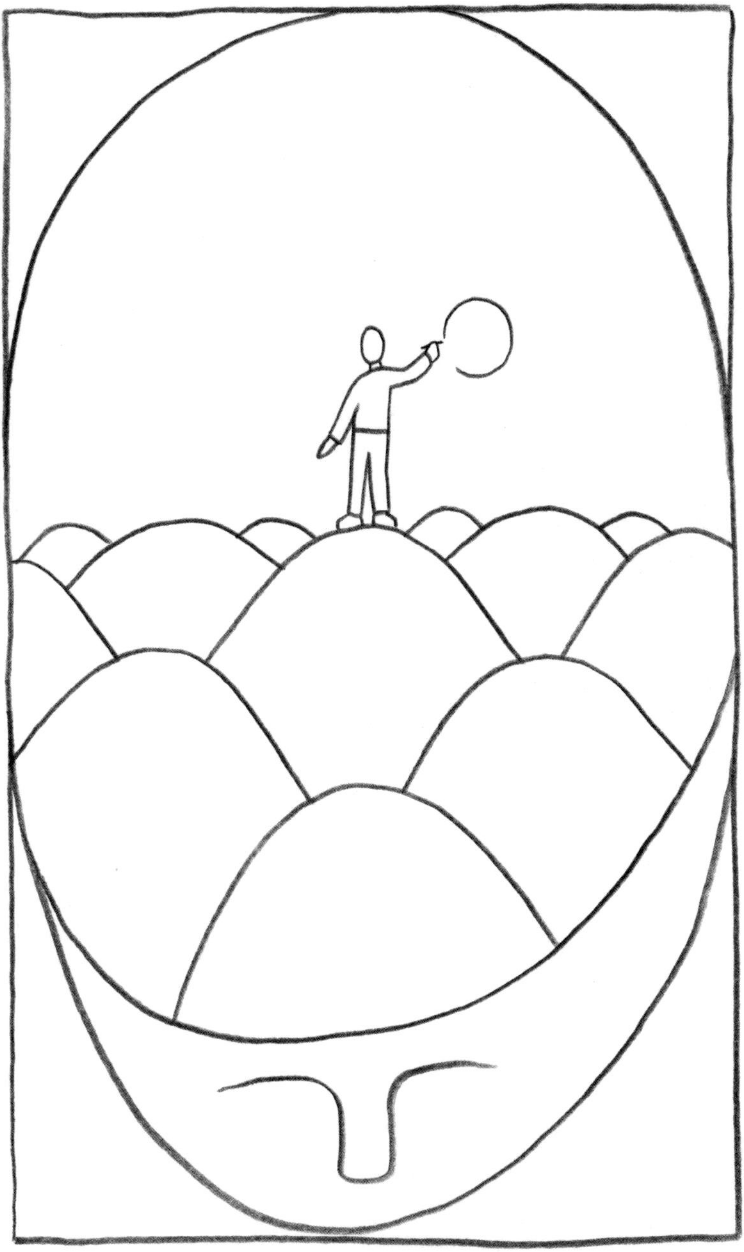

IN AN INSIGHTFUL BOOK AUTHORED BY POSITIVE PSYCHOLOGY RESEARCHER SONJA LYUBOMIRSKY, I STUMBLED UPON THE “SUSTAINABLE HAPPINESS MODEL.” ACCORDING TO THIS MODEL, OUR WELL-BEING IS SIGNIFICANTLY INFLUENCED BY OUR DAILY ACTIONS AND THOUGHTS.

INTENTIONAL ACTIVITIES CONTRIBUTE TO 40 PERCENT OF OUR HAPPINESS, WHILE GENETICS ACCOUNT FOR 50 PERCENT, AND LIFE CIRCUMSTANCES CONTRIBUTE MERELY 10 PERCENT.

THIS DISCOVERY WAS HEARTENING AND, FOR A WHILE, I BRIMMED WITH HOPE THAT IT MIGHT OFFER A SOLUTION TO MY BROTHER’S STRUGGLES.

BEFORE PASSING THE BOOK ON TO HIM, I TRIED TO INCORPORATE SOME OF THE DAILY ROUTINES AND PRACTICES MENTIONED THROUGHOUT ITS PAGES INTO MY OWN LIFE.

OVER TIME, I INDEED EXPERIENCED A MODEST INCREASE IN HAPPINESS.

HOWEVER, I ALSO CAME TO RECOGNIZE THE CHALLENGE OF STICKING TO THOSE ROUTINES – A CHALLENGE THAT BECOMES EVEN MORE INTRICATE FOR PEOPLE GRAPPLING WITH MENTAL ILLNESS.

40 %

INTENTIONAL ACTIVITIES
that include practices like gratitude, acts of kindness, mindfulness, physical exercise, nurturing social connections, and setting and pursuing goals, all of which actively contribute to increasing and maintaining happiness over time.

10 %

LIFE CIRCUMSTANCES OR EXTERNAL FACTORS
like income, career, relationships, health, or other life events. While they can have a significant impact on our well-being, their effect is often temporary, as we tend to adapt to new circumstances over time, returning to our baseline level of happiness.

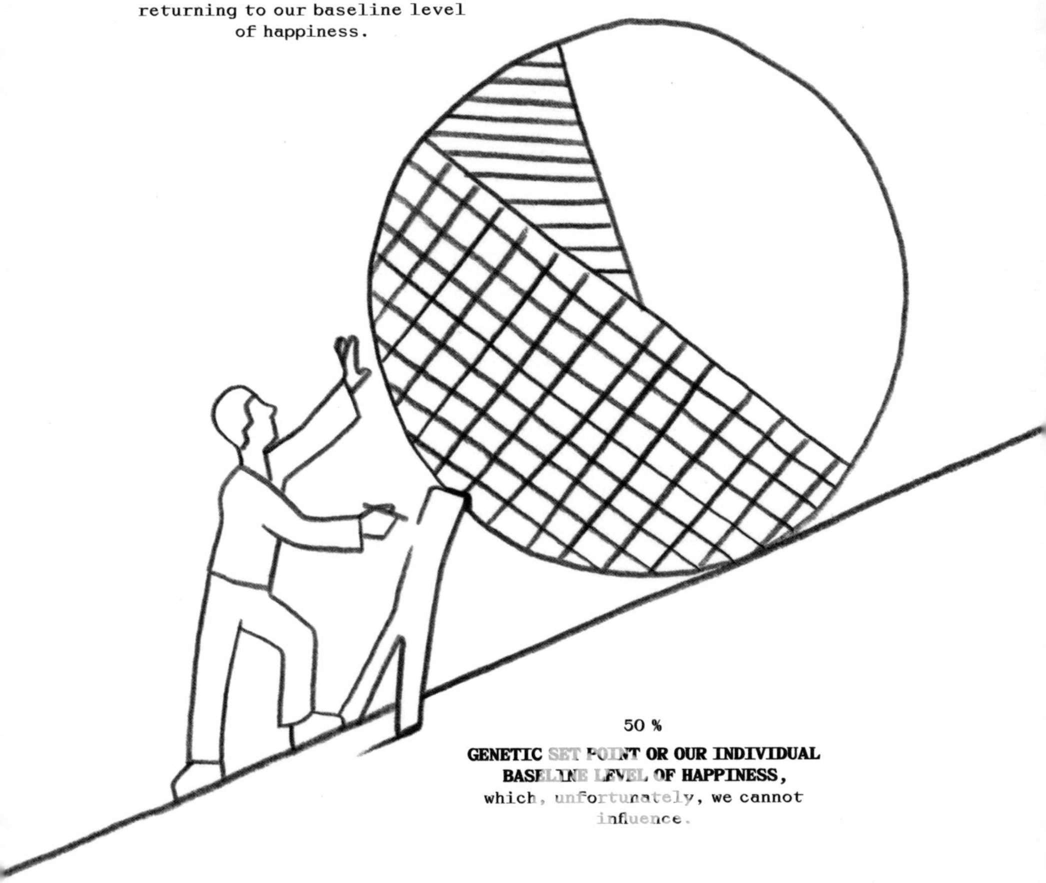

50 %

GENETIC SET POINT OR OUR INDIVIDUAL BASELINE LEVEL OF HAPPINESS,
which, unfortunately, we cannot influence.

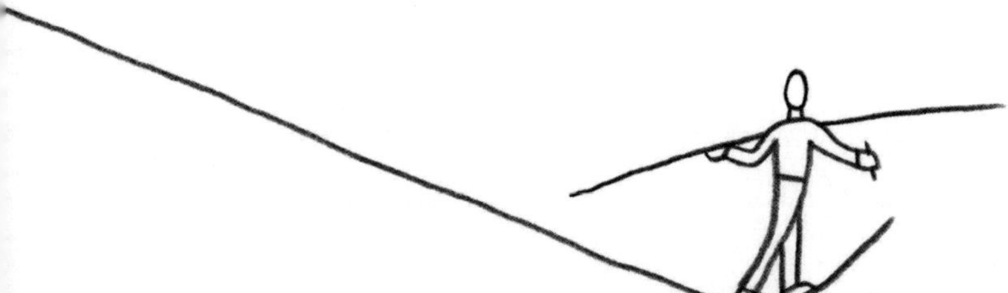

AROUND THAT TIME,
I BEGAN TO FILL MY SKETCHBOOKS WITH DRAWINGS
POPULATED BY FIGURES
WHO FEARLESSLY
CHALLENGE THE BOUNDARIES OF THEIR REALITIES,
EQUIPPED ONLY WITH A PENCIL IN HAND.

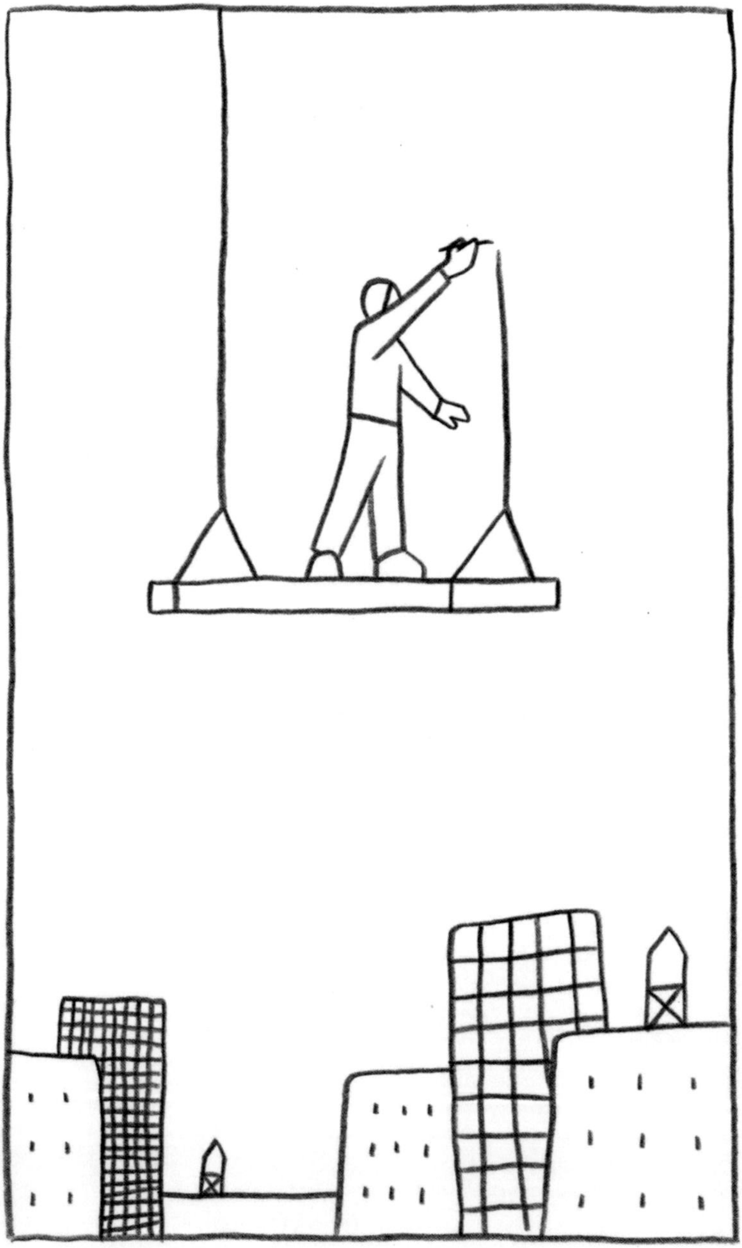

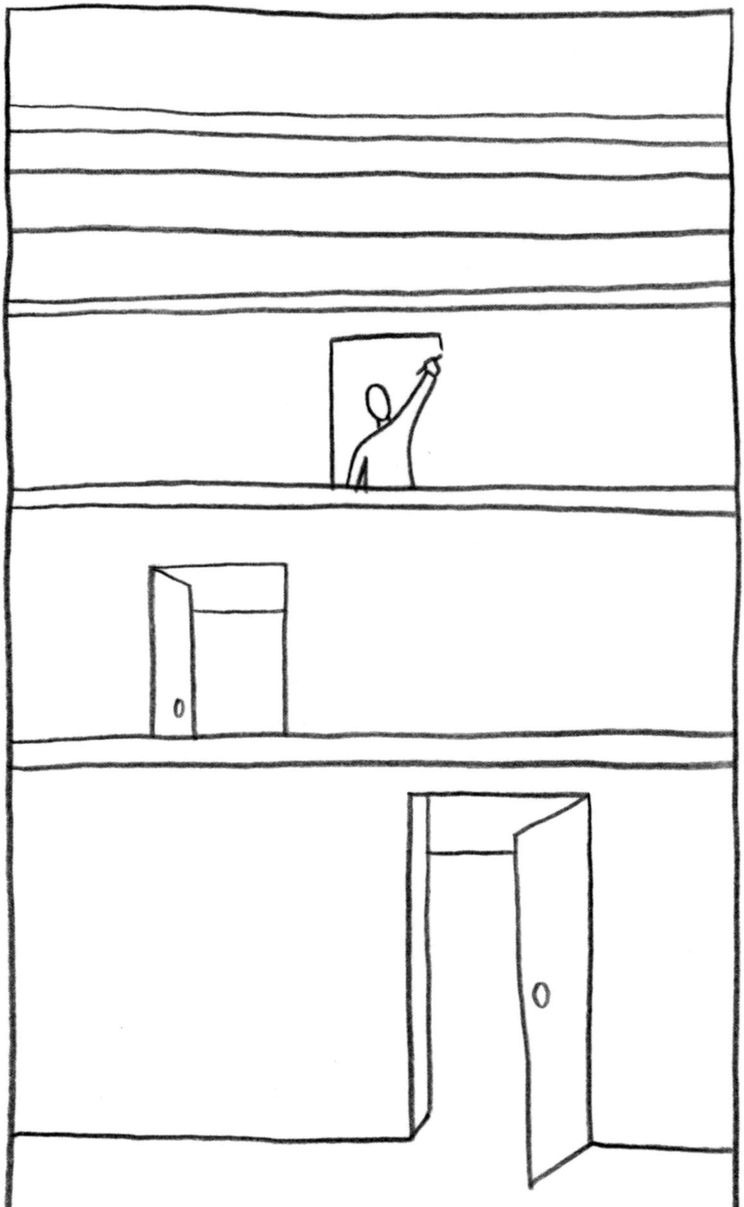

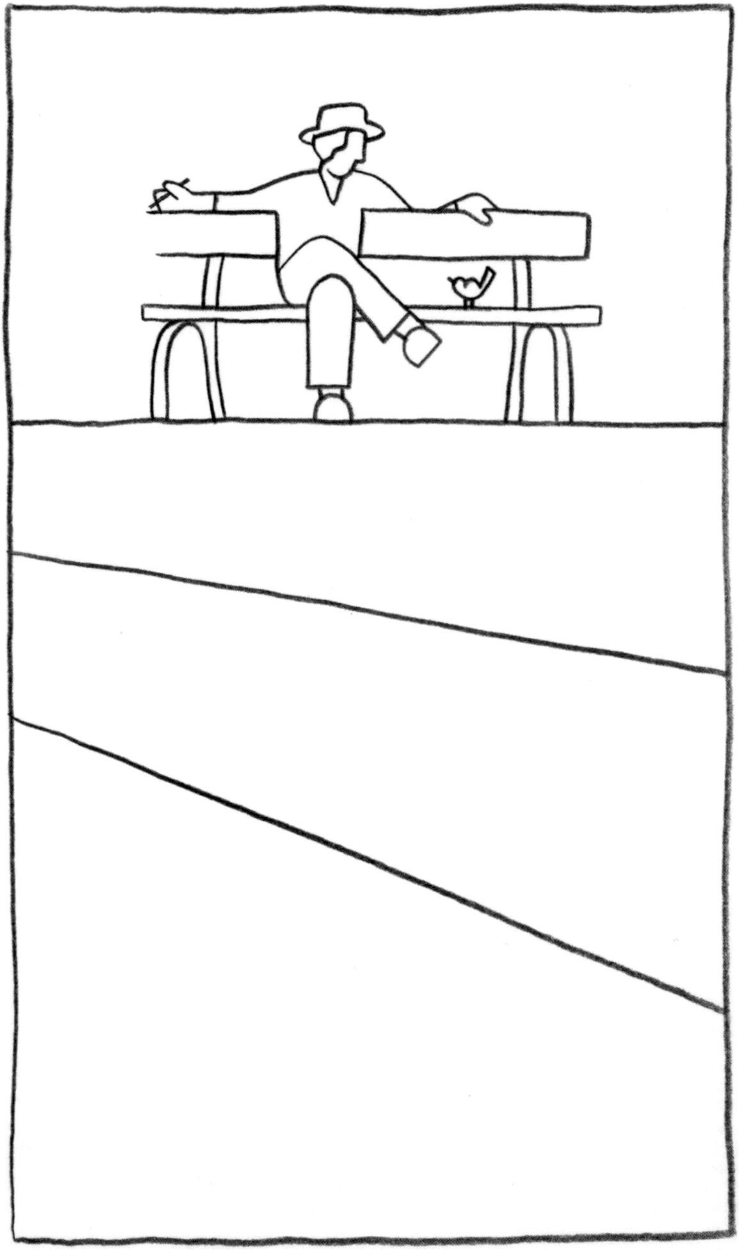

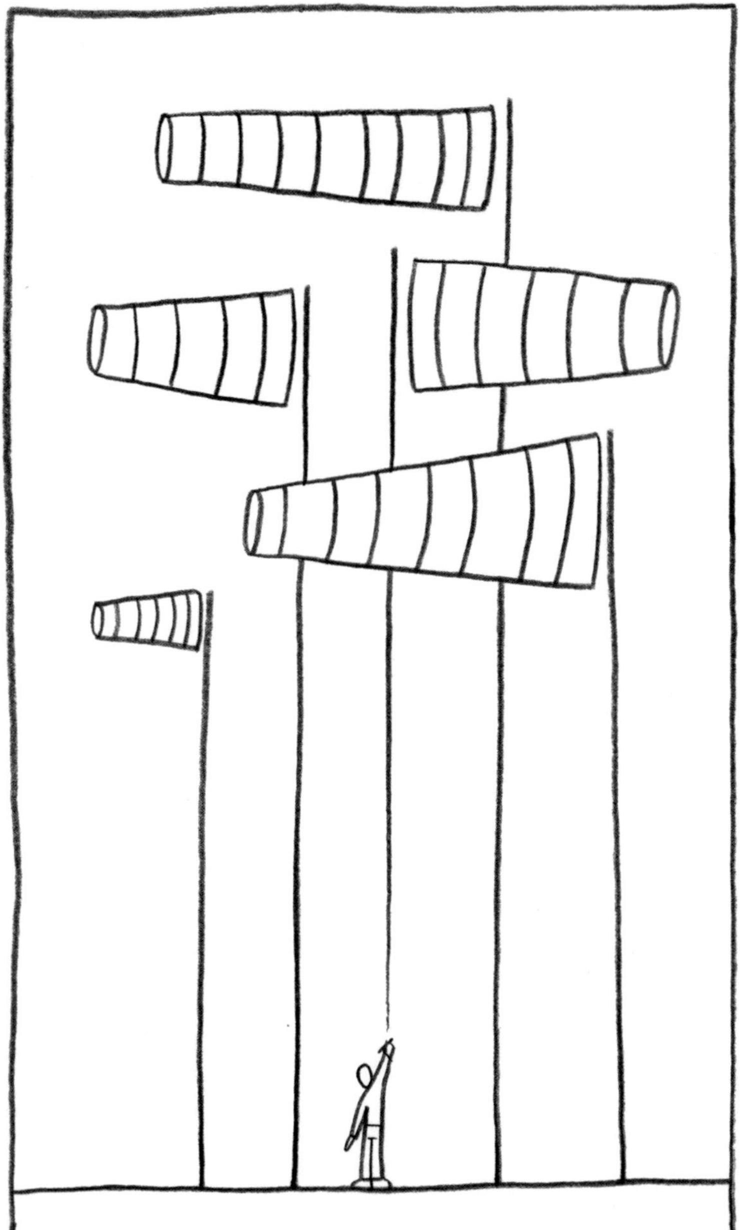

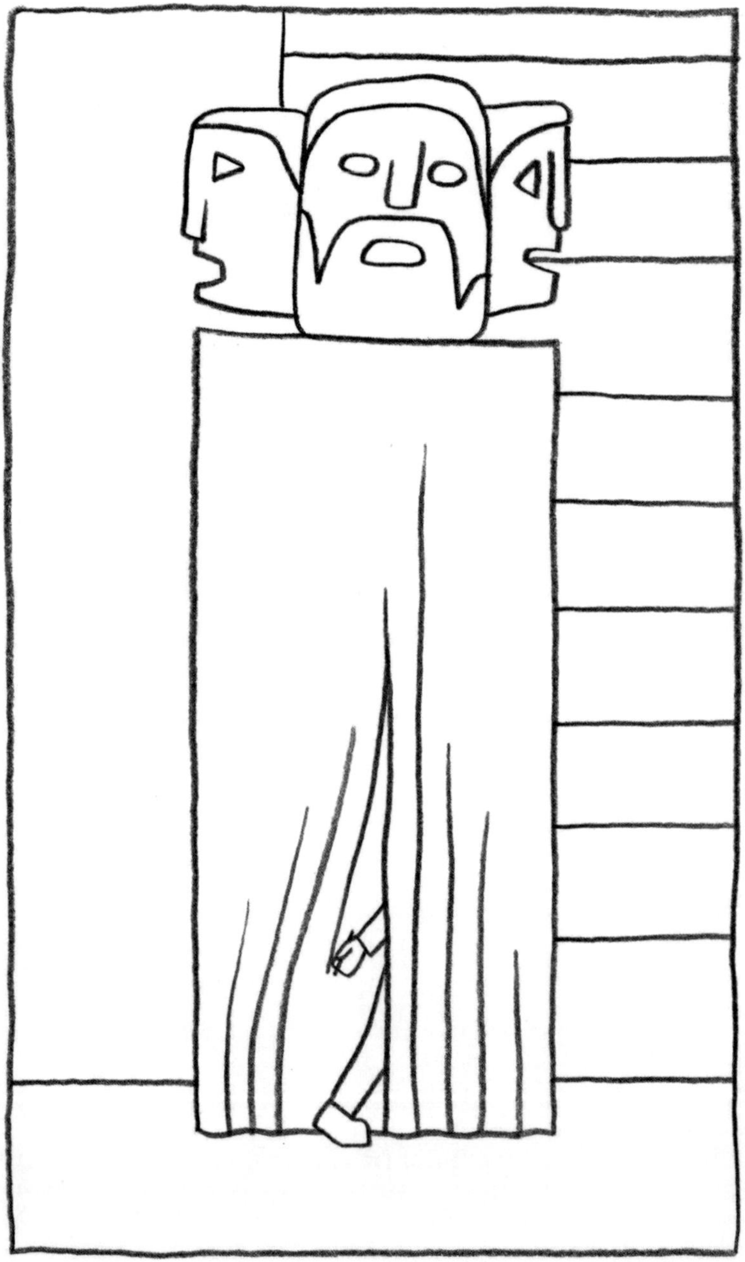

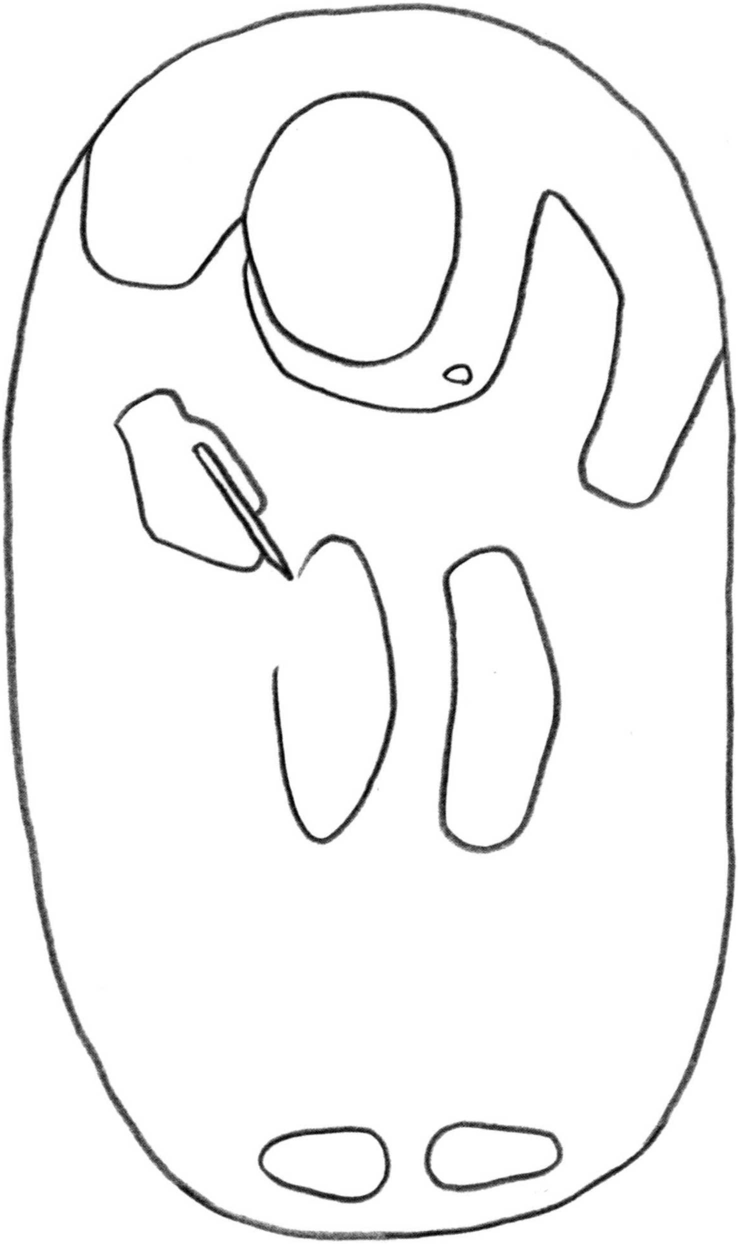

I FELT INSECURE ABOUT THEIR MEANING
FOR YEARS, YET THEY CONTINUED TO EMERGE.

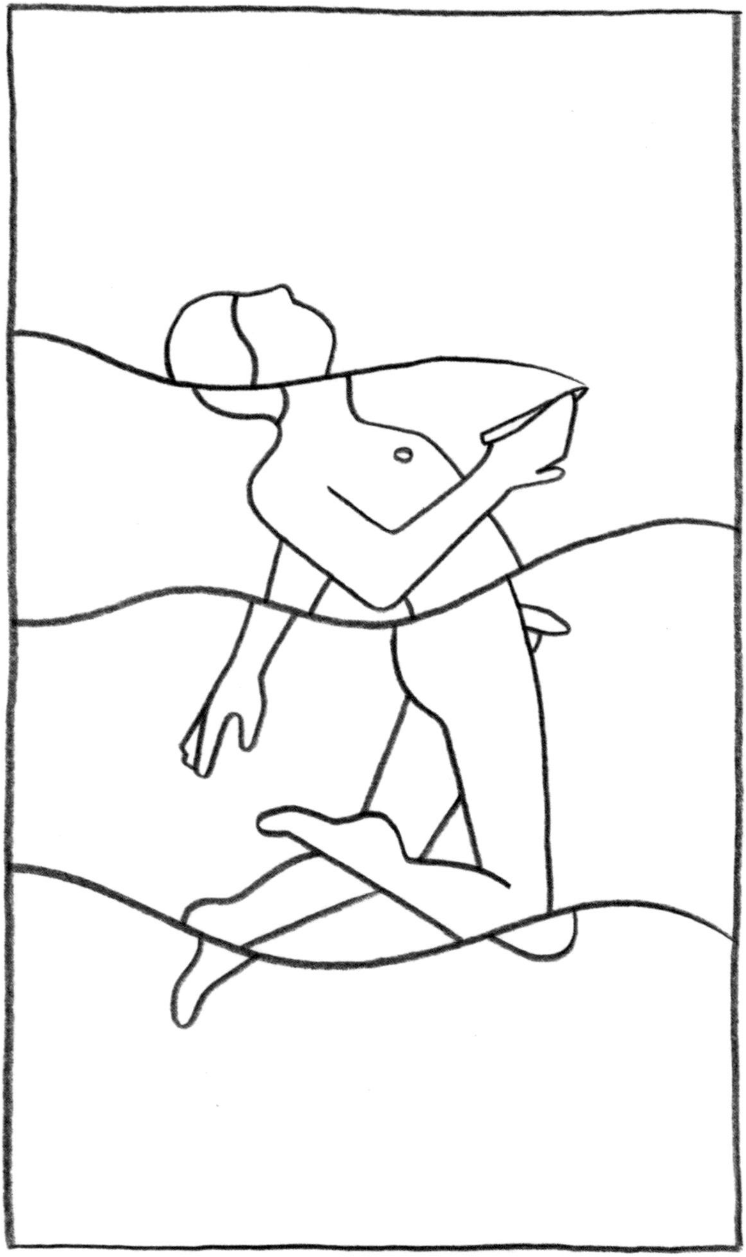

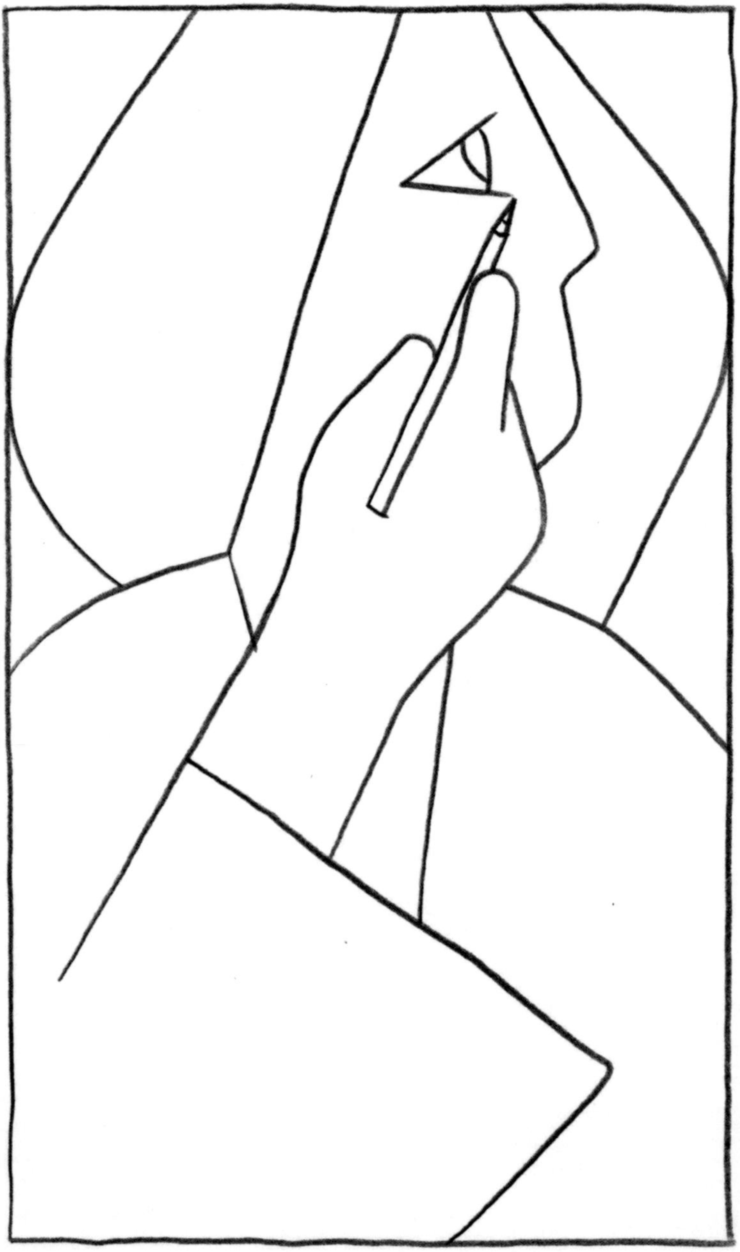

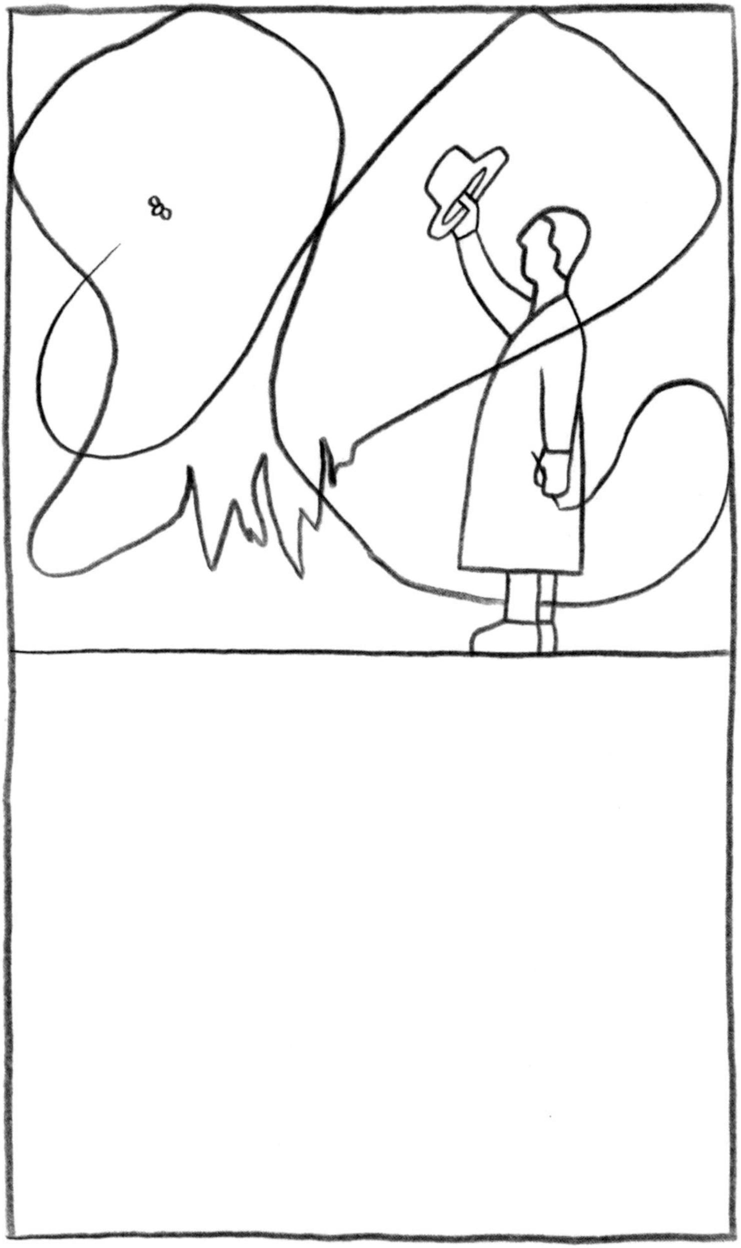

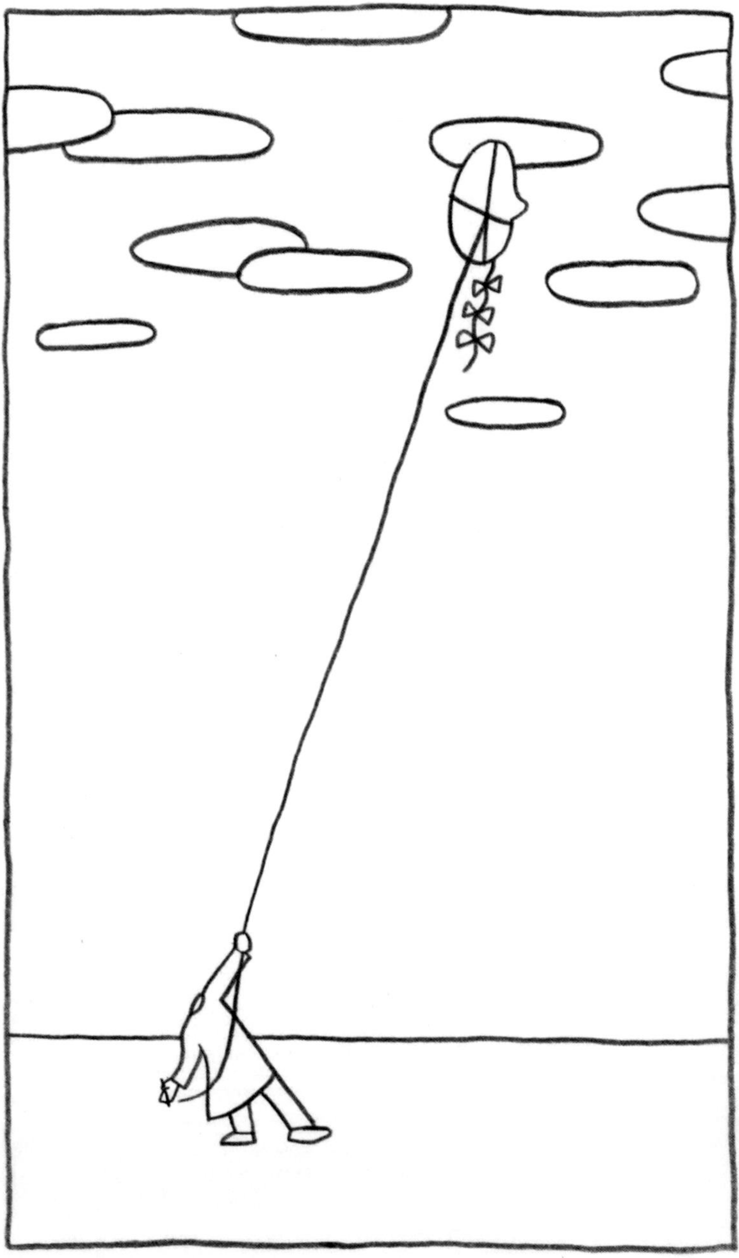

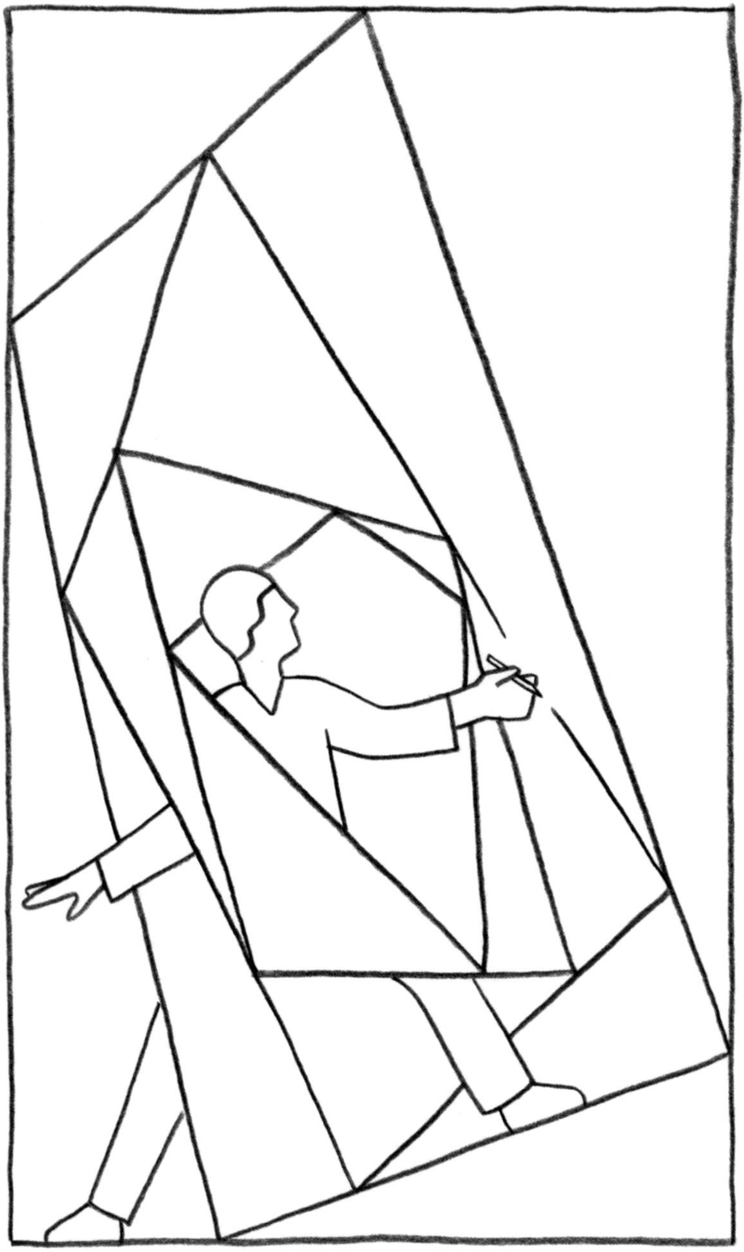

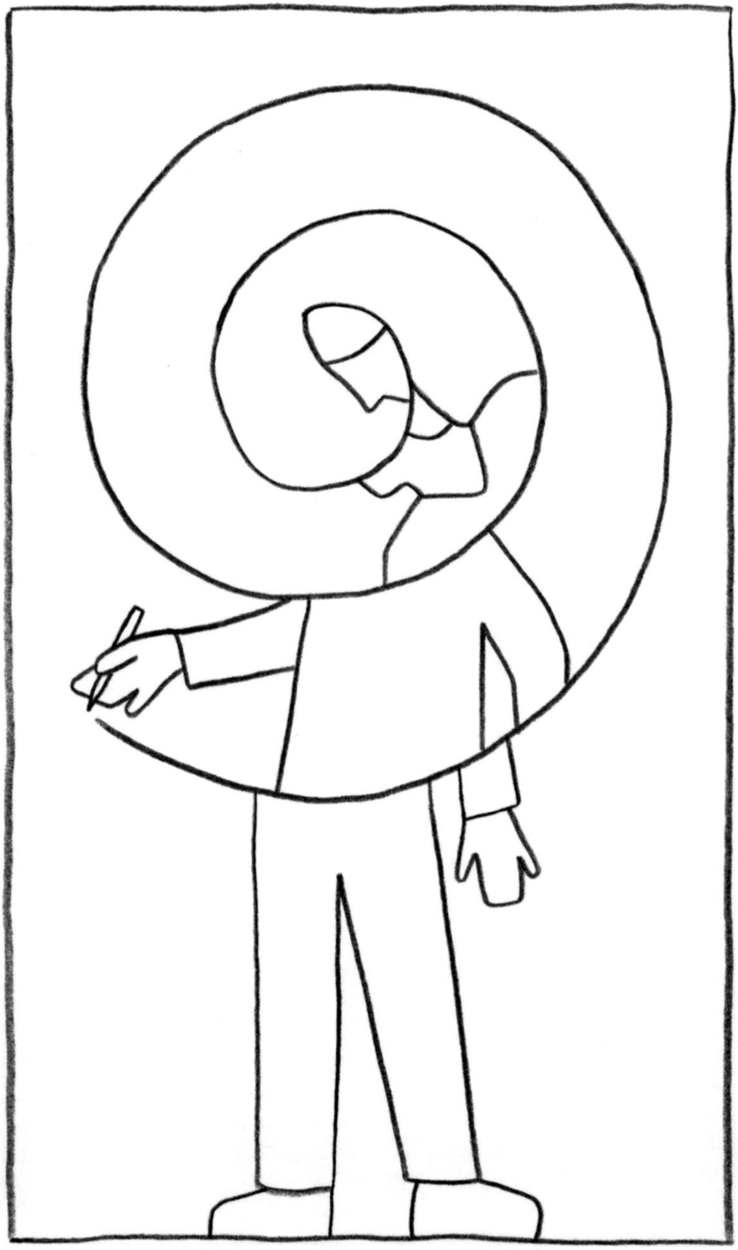

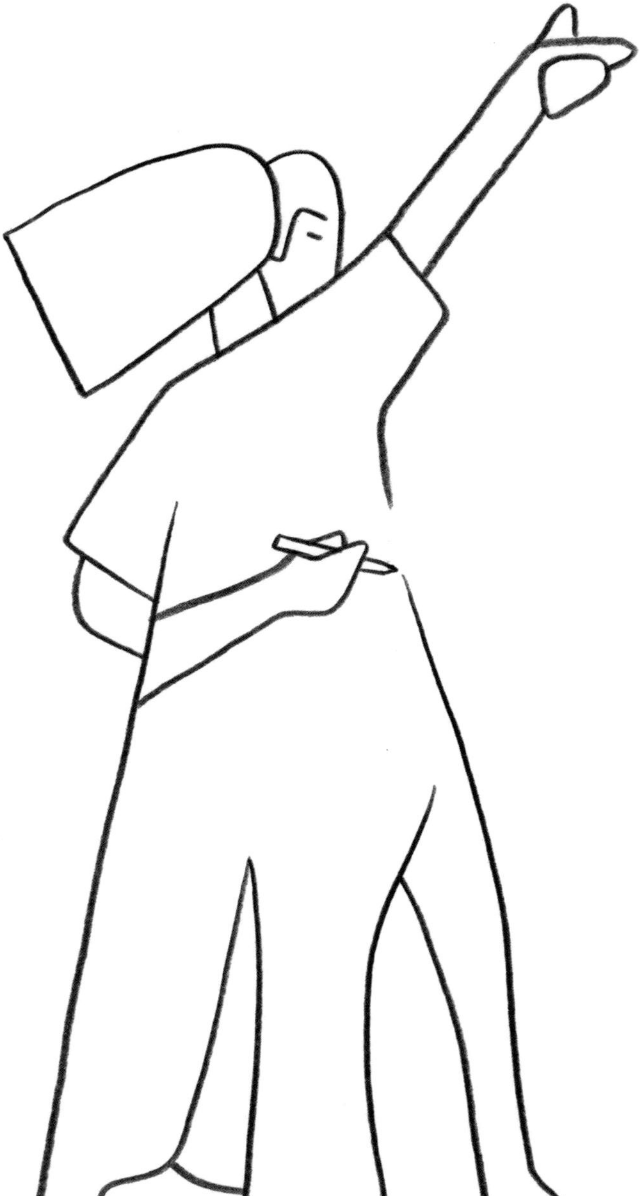

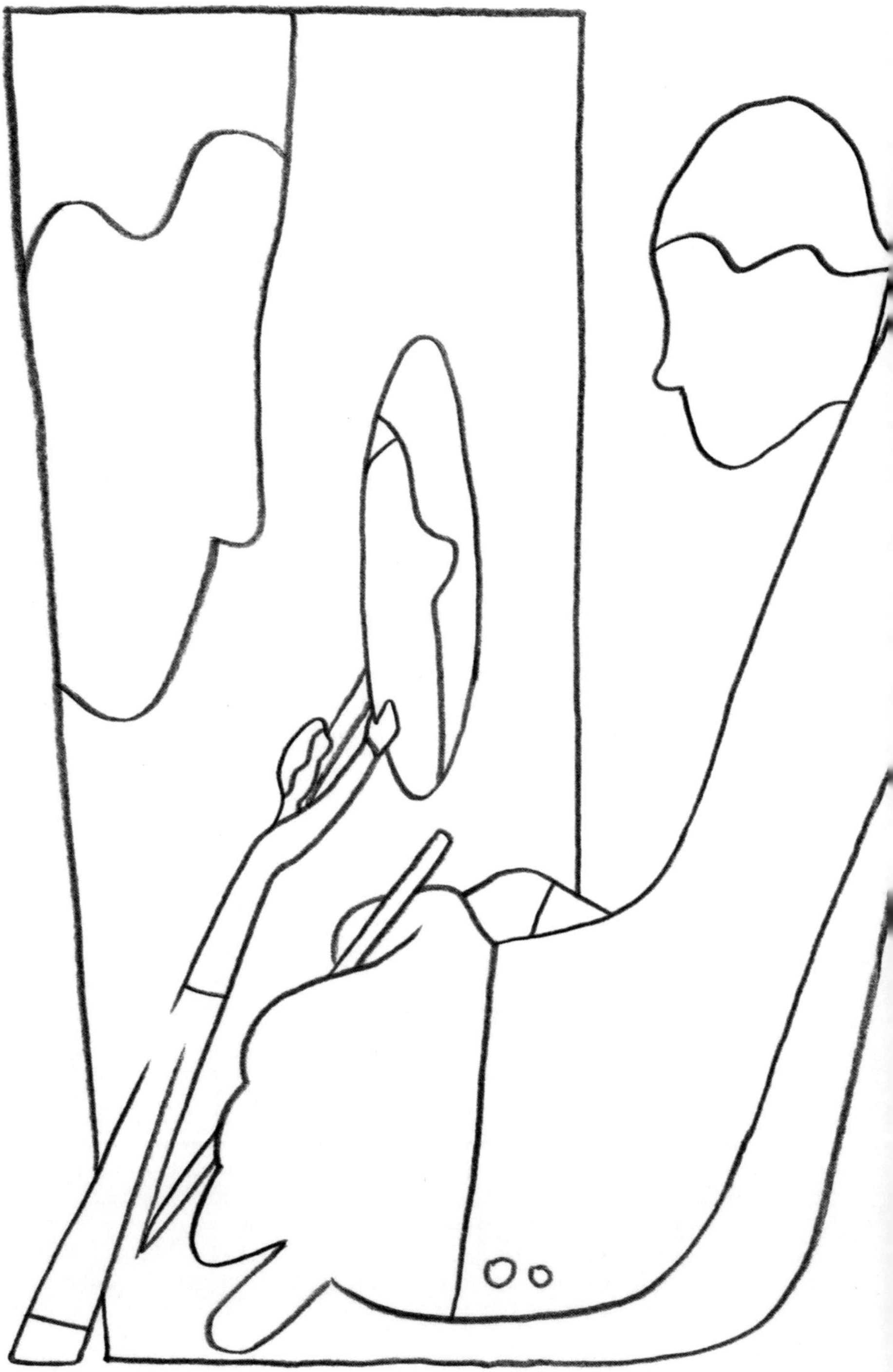

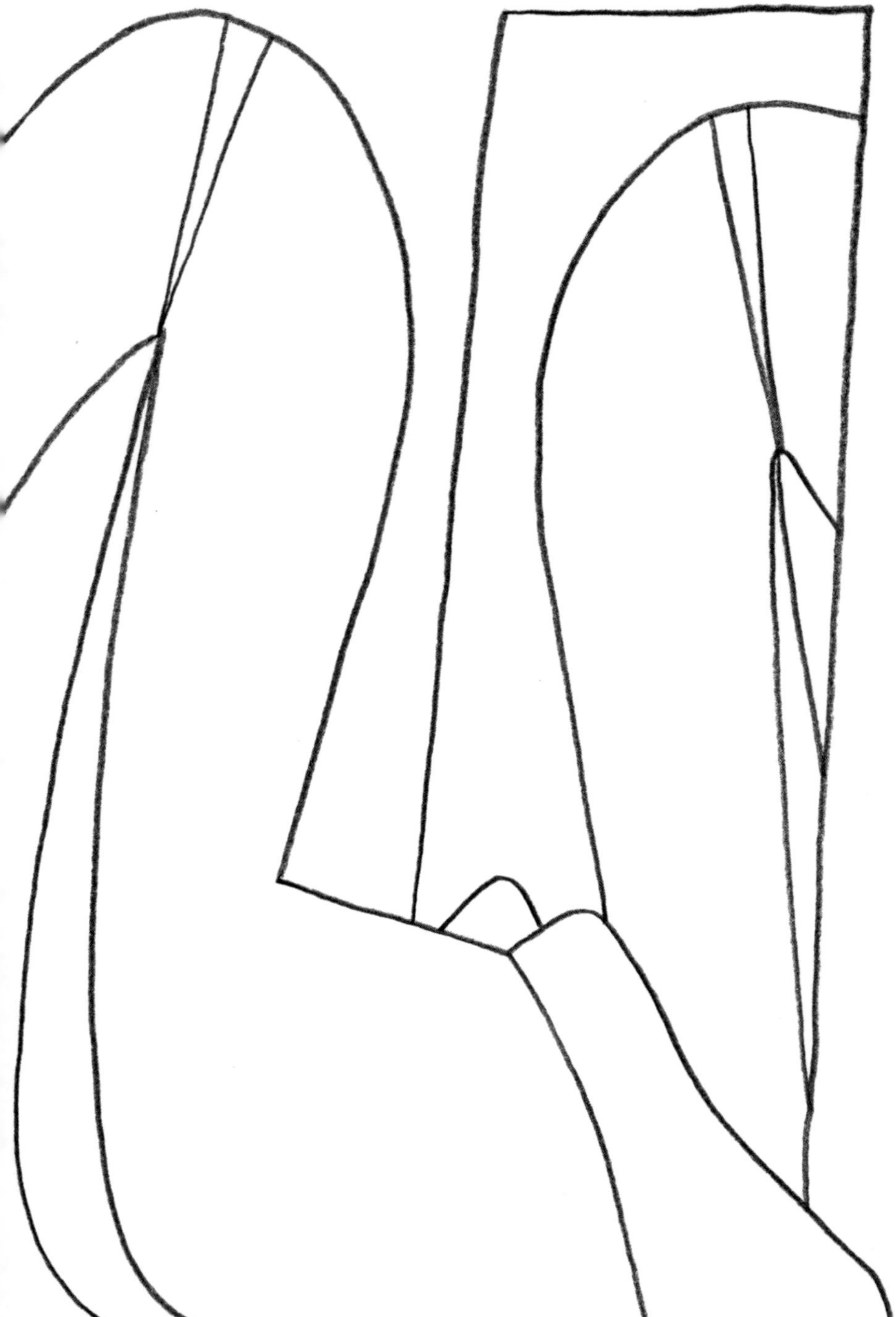

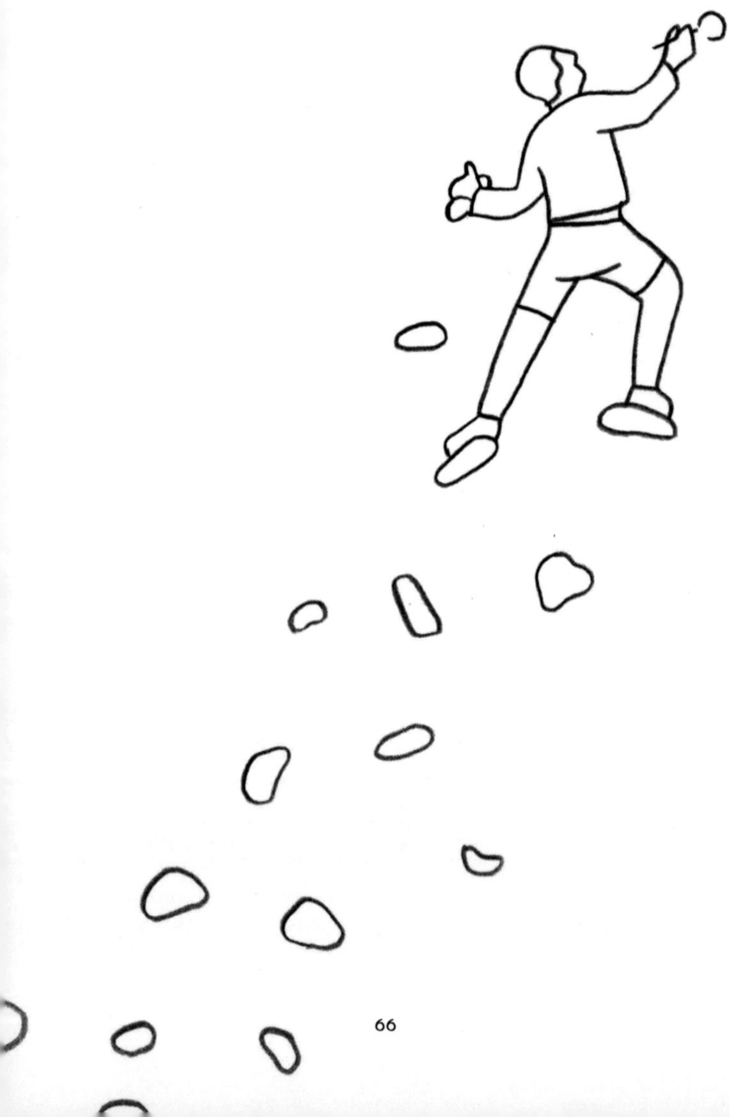

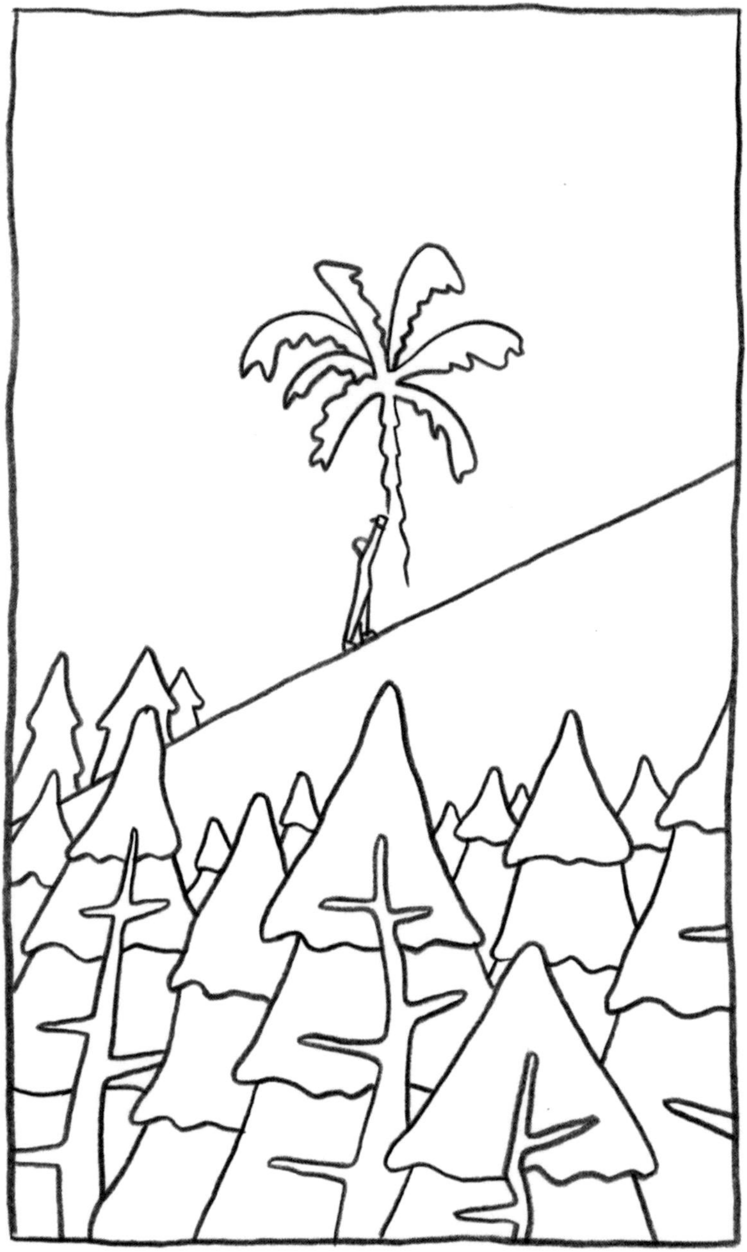

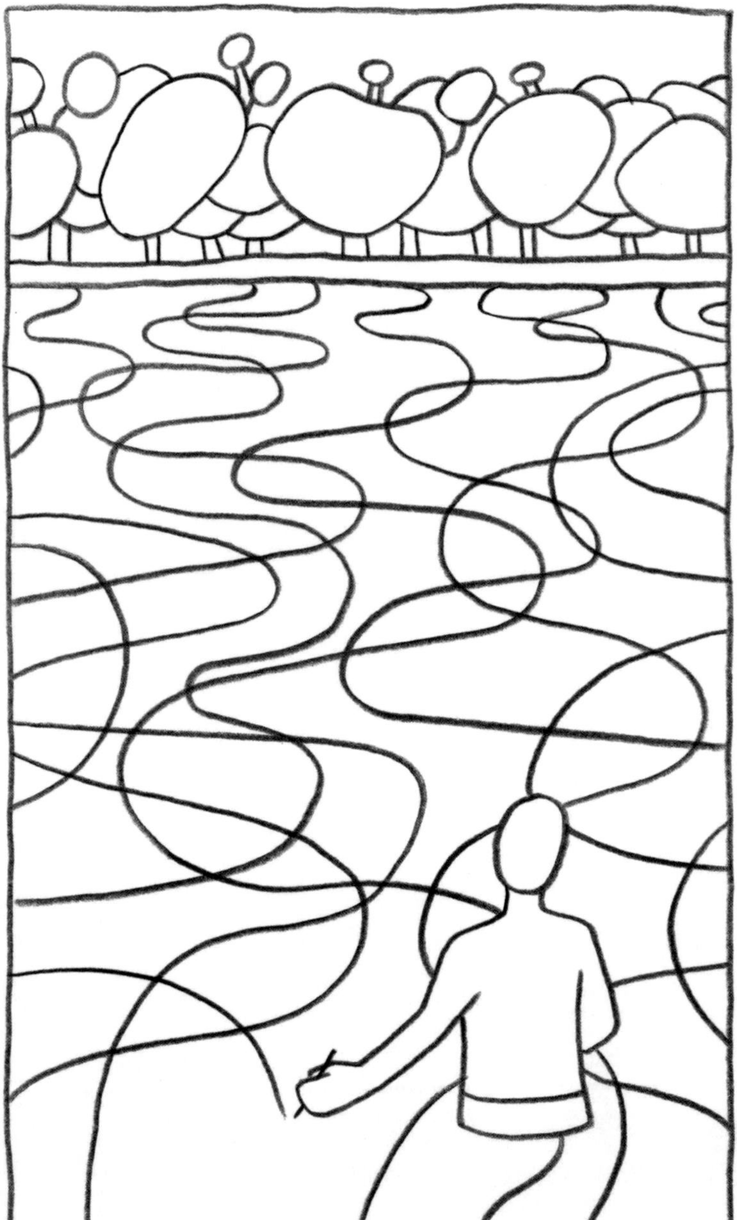

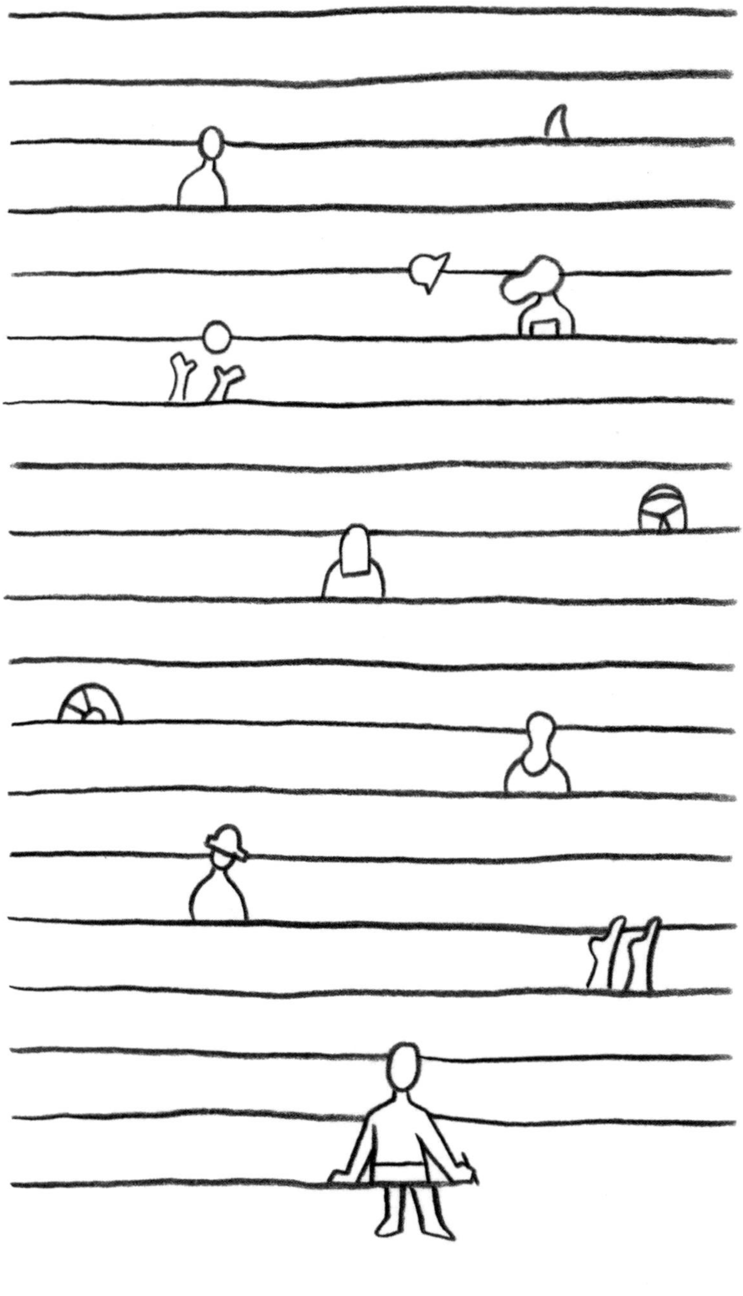

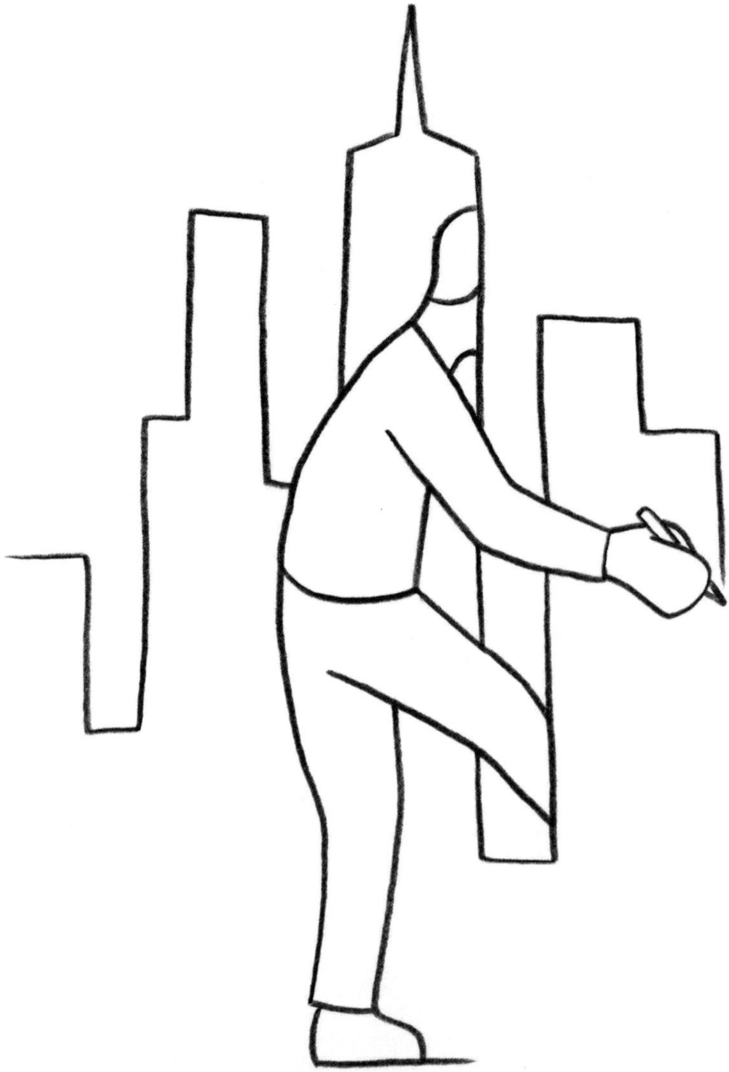

WHENEVER AND WHEREVER I COULD,
I ADDED TO MY SKETCHBOOKS.

FOLLOWING MY BROTHER'S ATTEMPT,
I TRAVELED EXTENSIVELY UNTIL, AT SOME POINT,
A DEAR FRIEND ASKED ME
IF I WAS SIMPLY CURIOUS TO SEE THE WORLD
OR IF I WAS TRYING TO ESCAPE FROM SOMETHING.

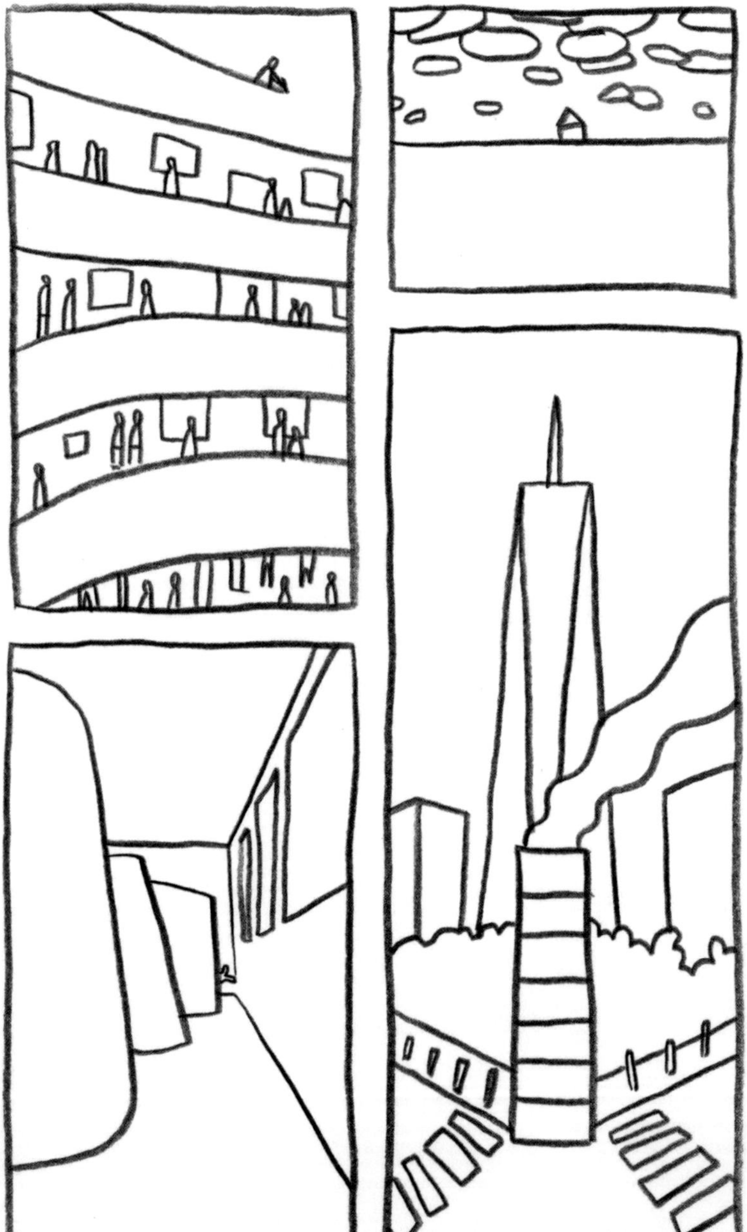

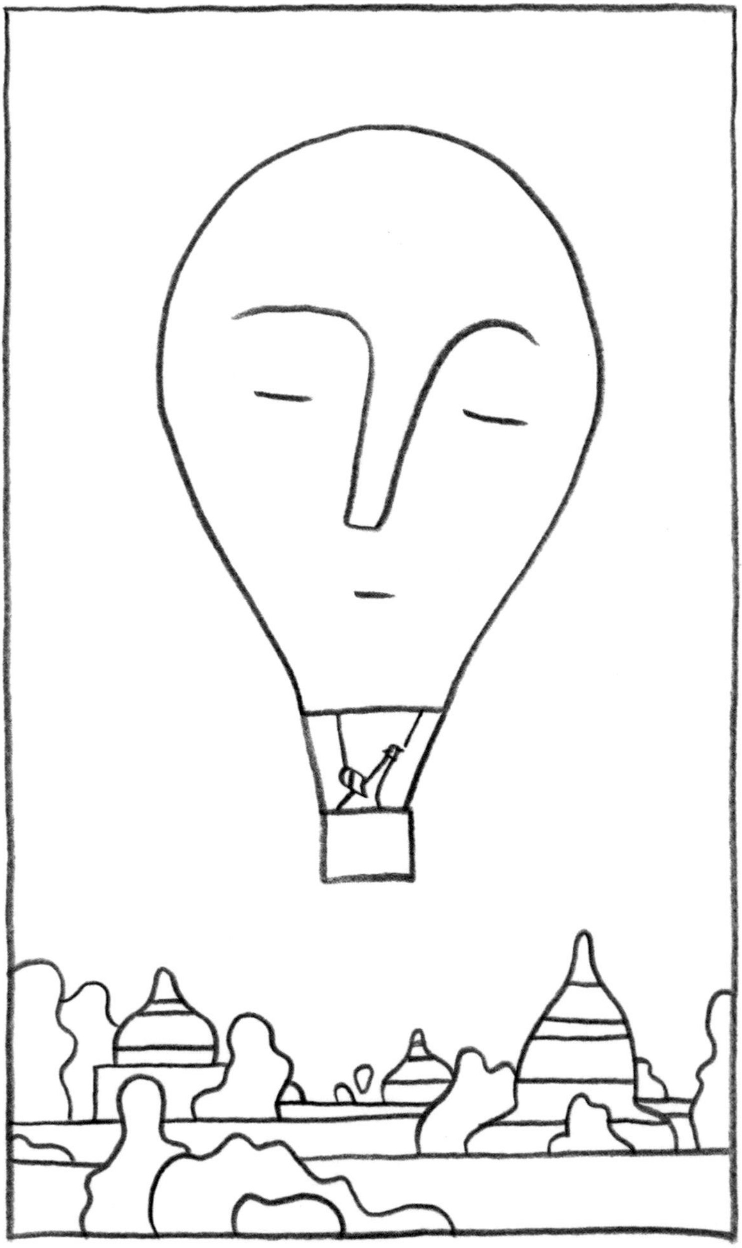

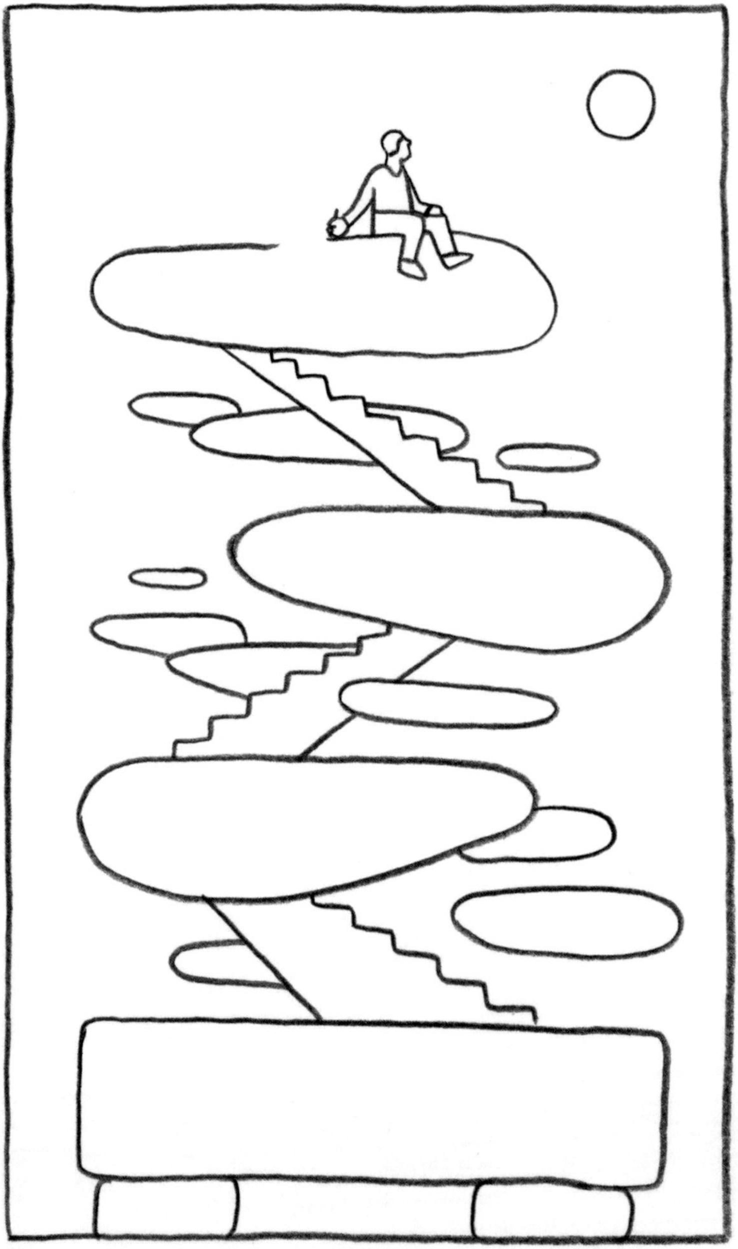

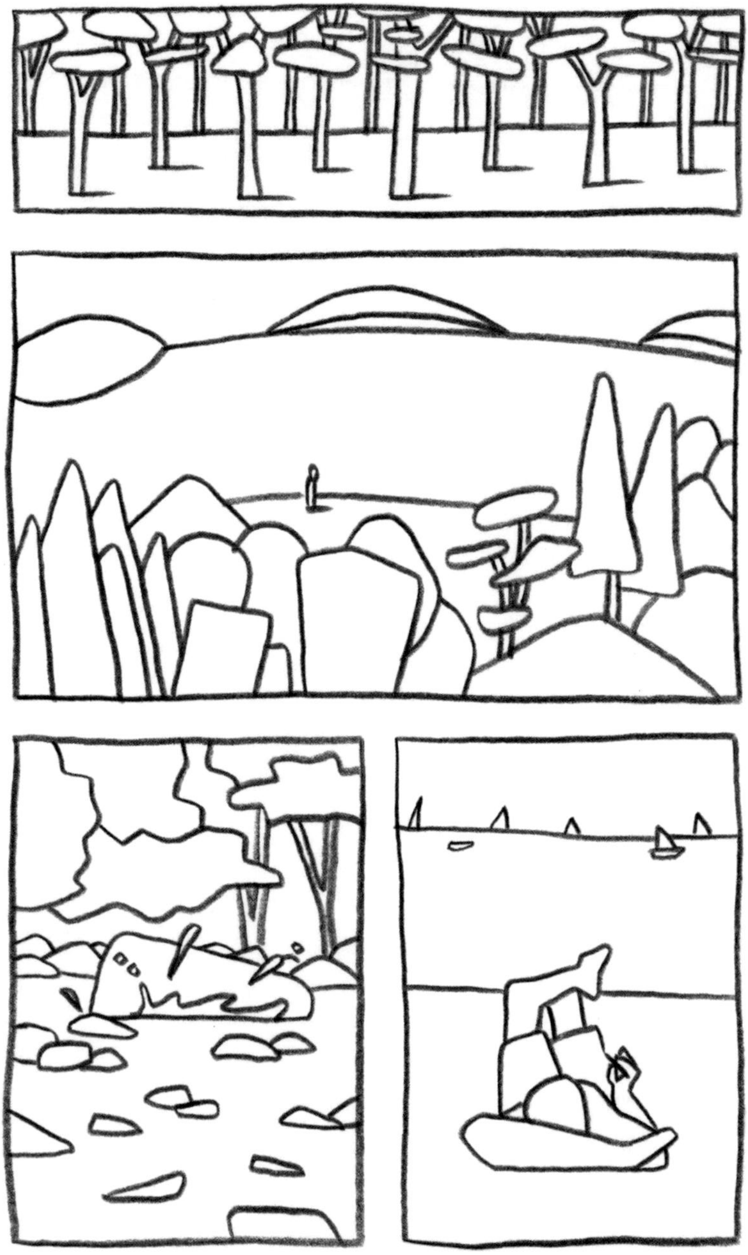

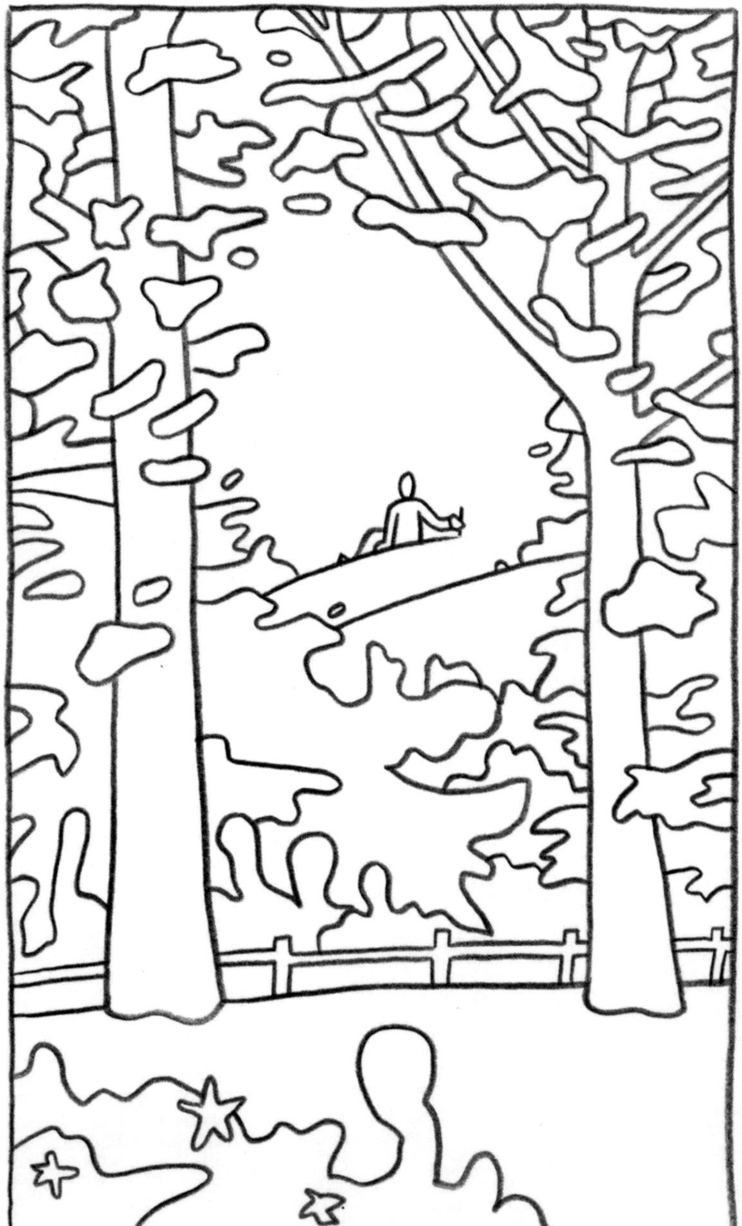

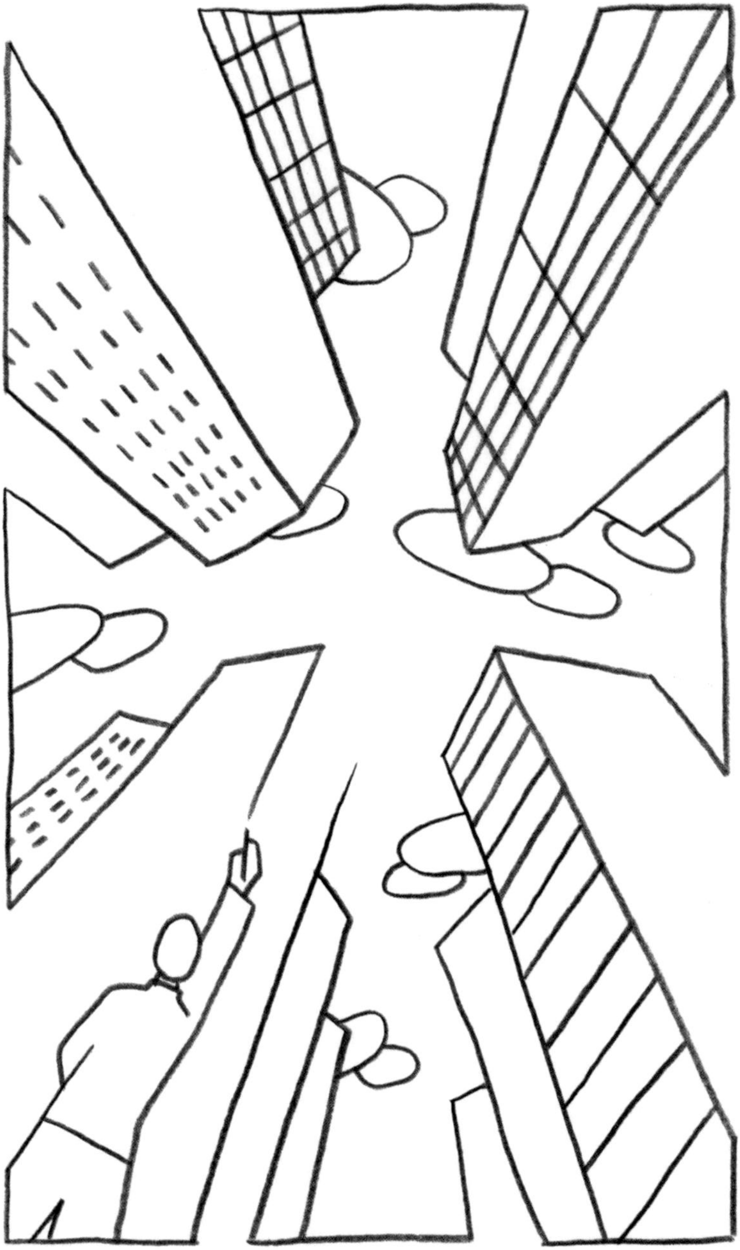

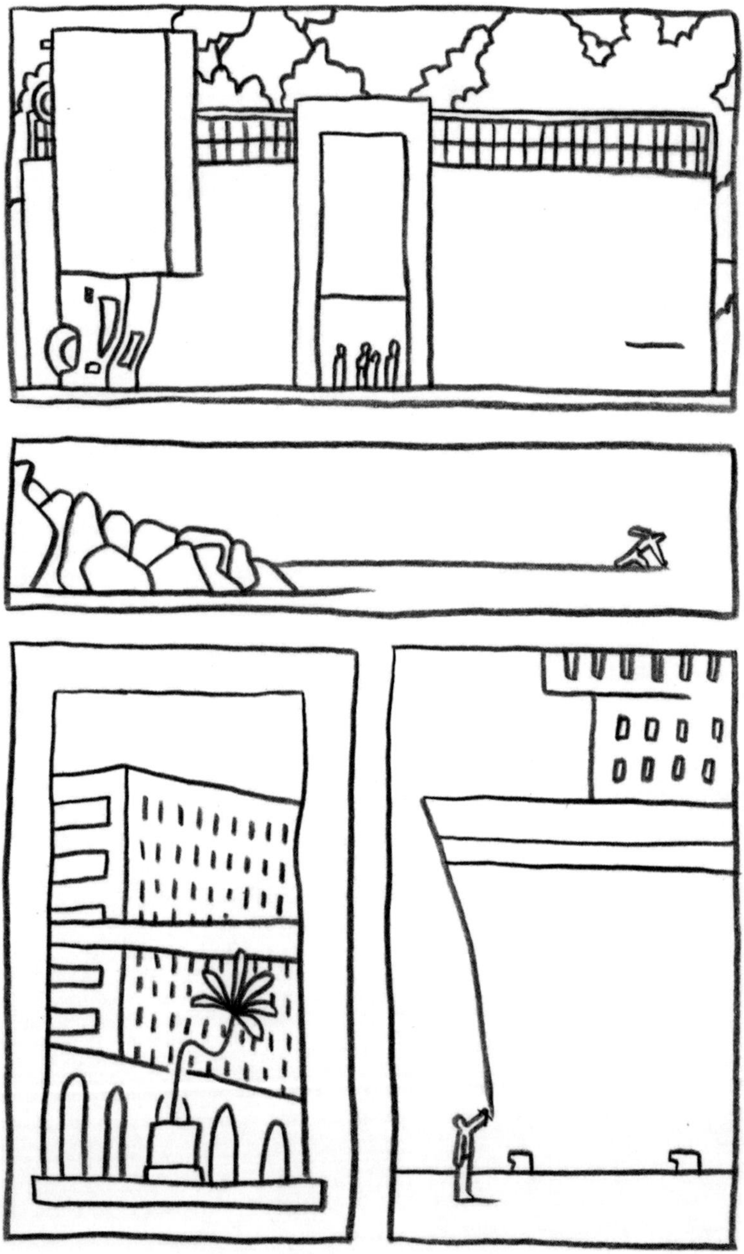

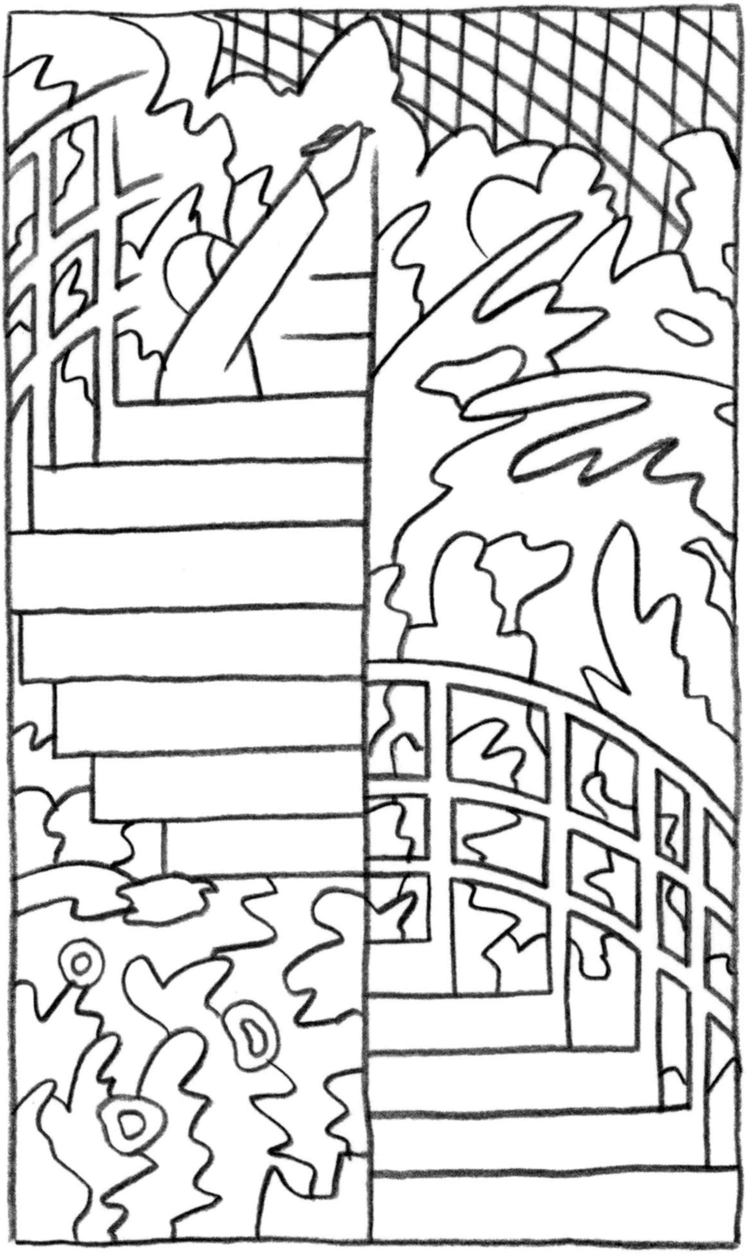

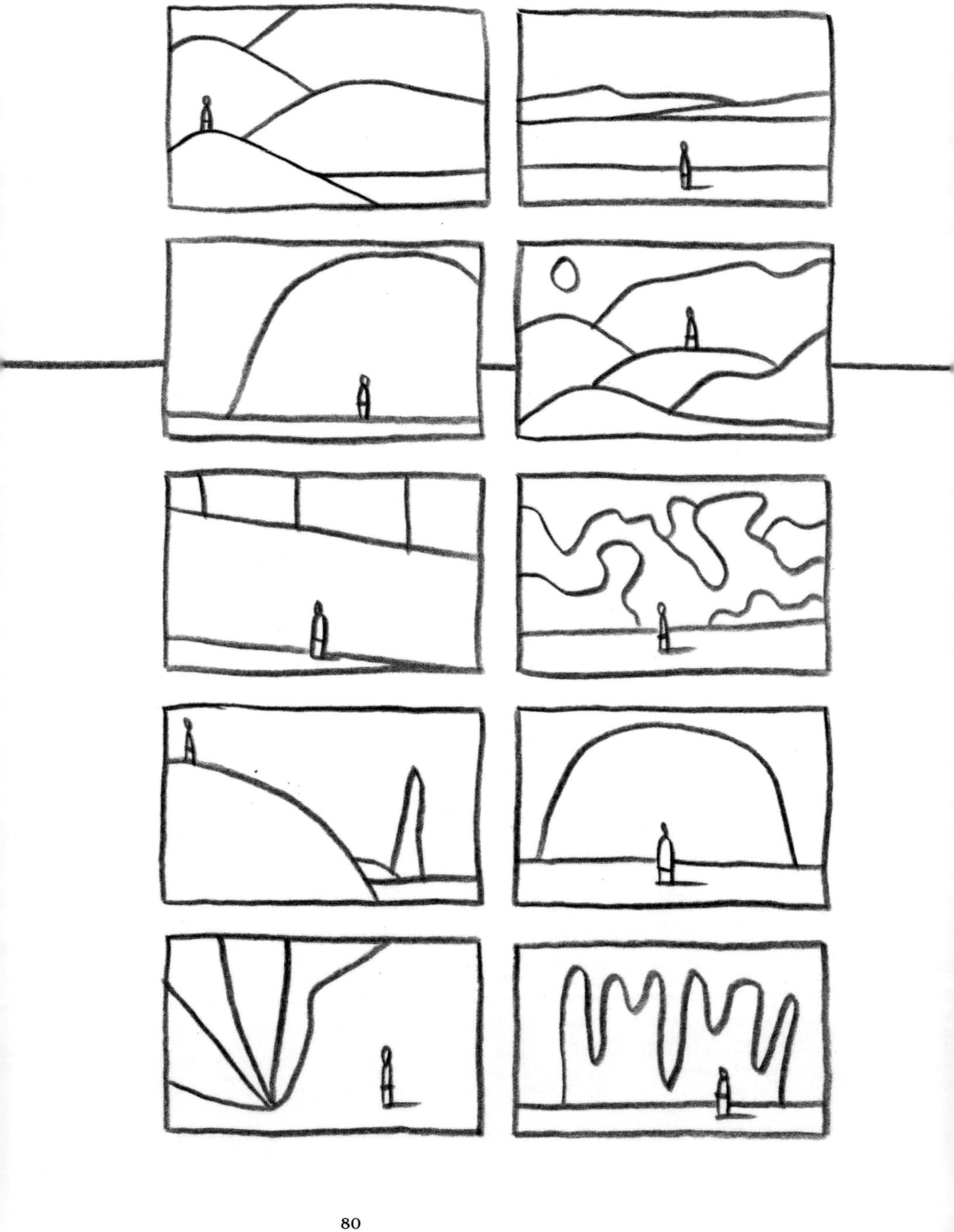

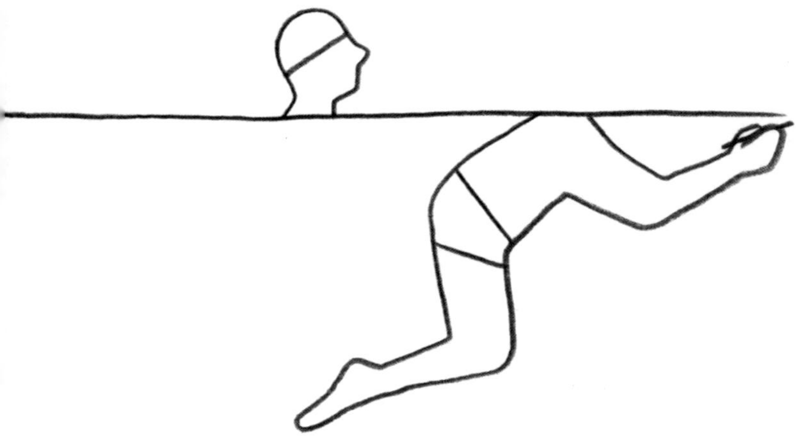

AT FIRST, I THOUGHT THAT
ALL THESE DRAWINGS WERE SIMPLY ABOUT DRAWING.

ABOUT GENERATING IDEAS
AND THINKING WITH THE HANDS.

ABOUT ILLUSTRATION,
THE PROFESSION I HAVE CHOSEN.

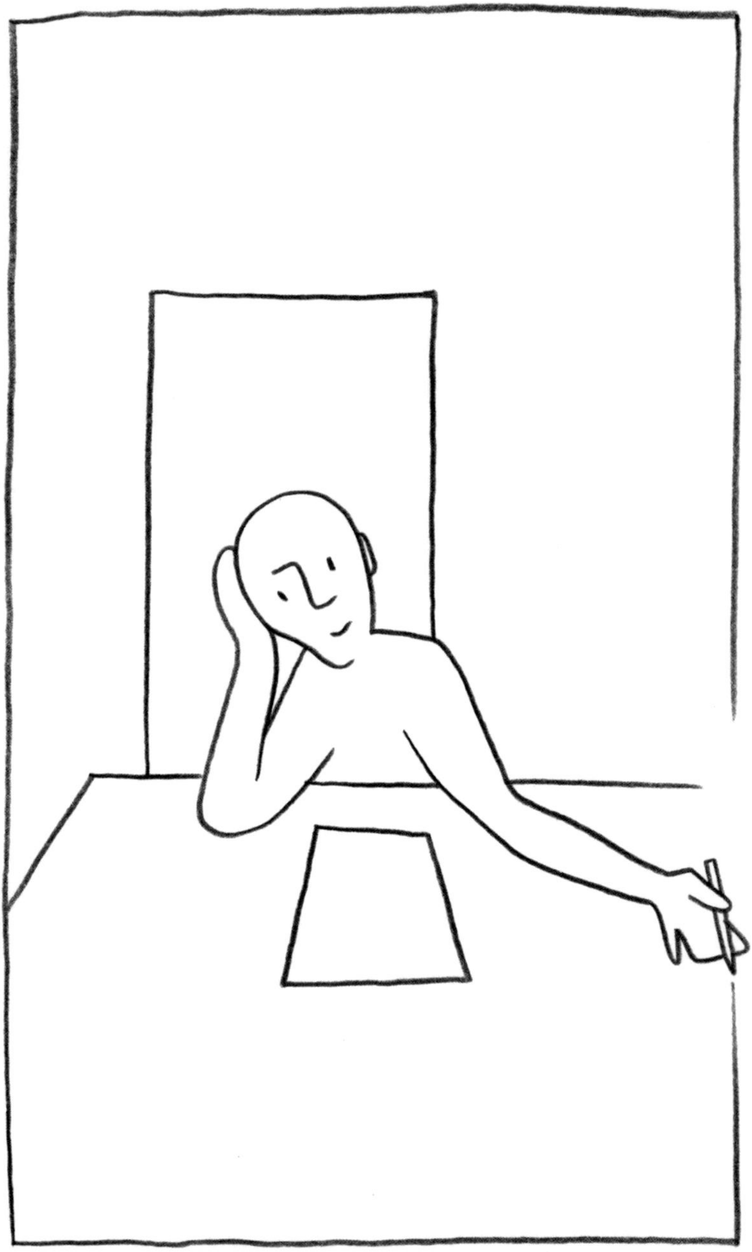

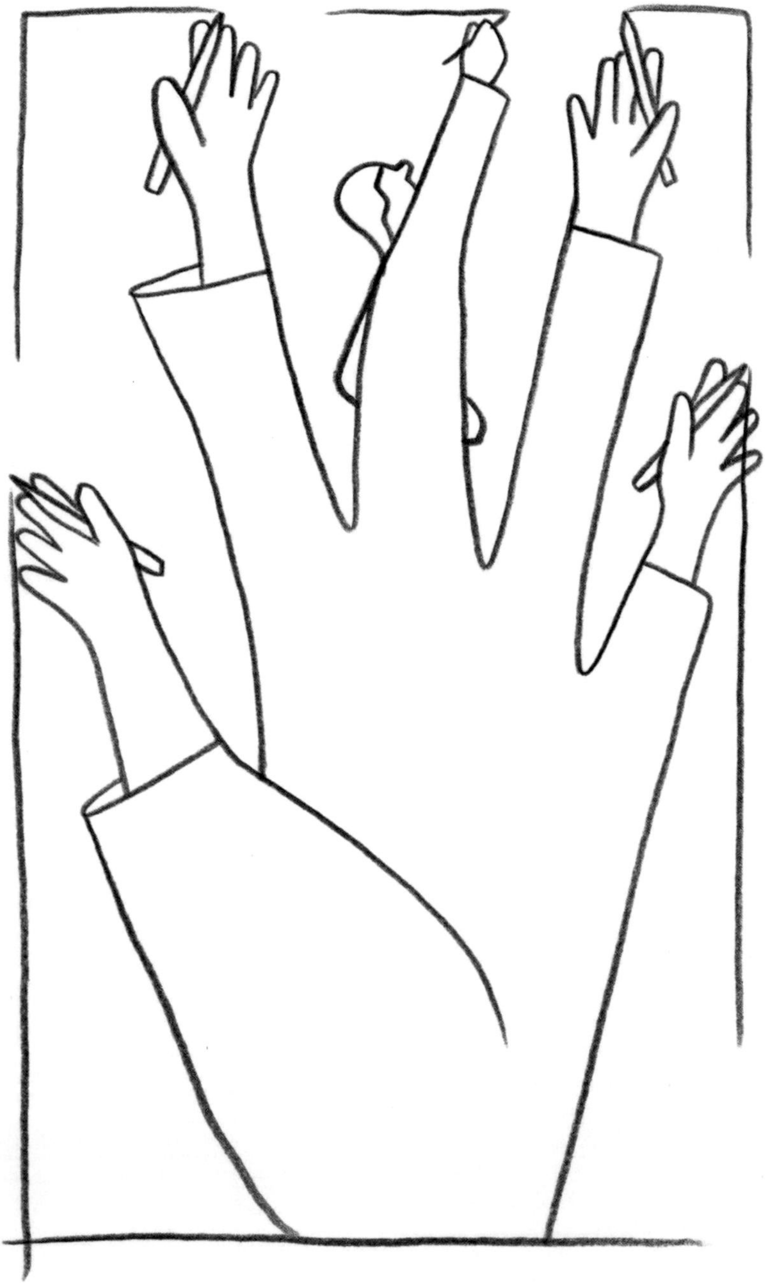

SURPRISED BY THE VAST AMOUNT OF THEMES
THESE DRAWINGS OF DRAWING FIGURES COULD CONVEY,
I SOLD SOME OF THEM TO NEWSPAPERS AND MAGAZINES
TO ILLUSTRATE STORIES OF ALL KINDS,
WRITTEN BY OTHERS.

LITTLE DID I SUSPECT
THAT THEY WERE TELLING YET ANOTHER STORY
IN THEIR OWN RIGHT.

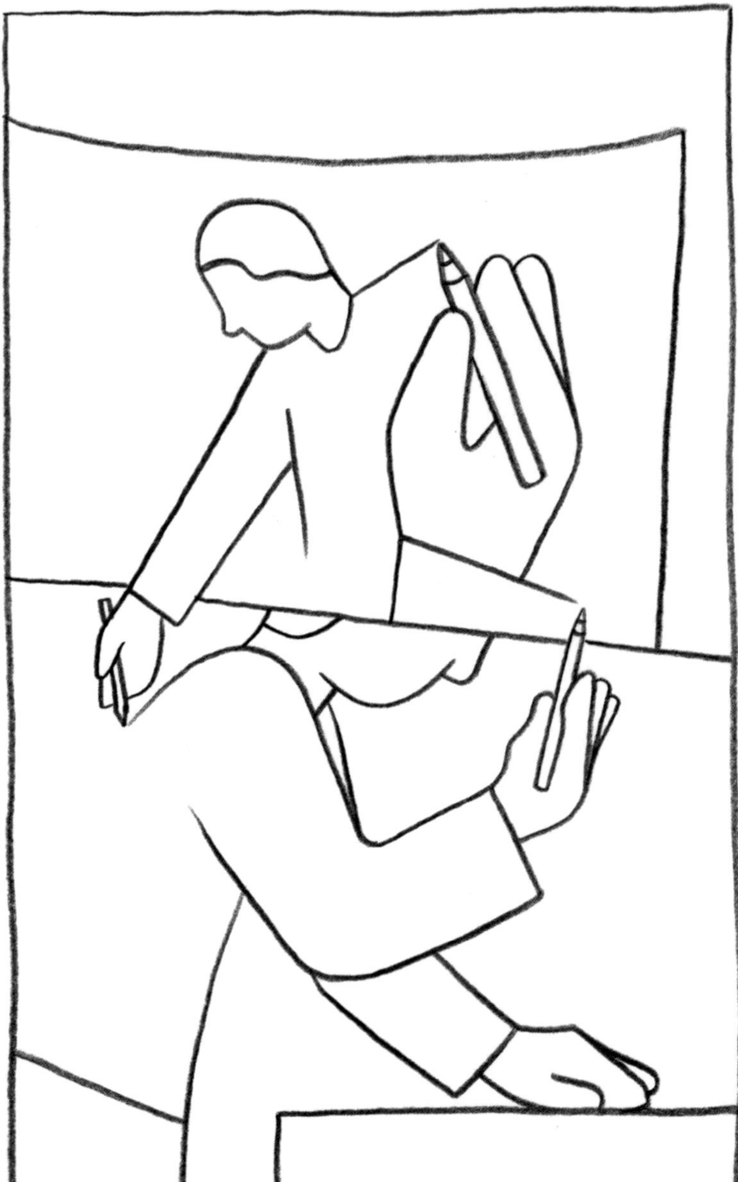

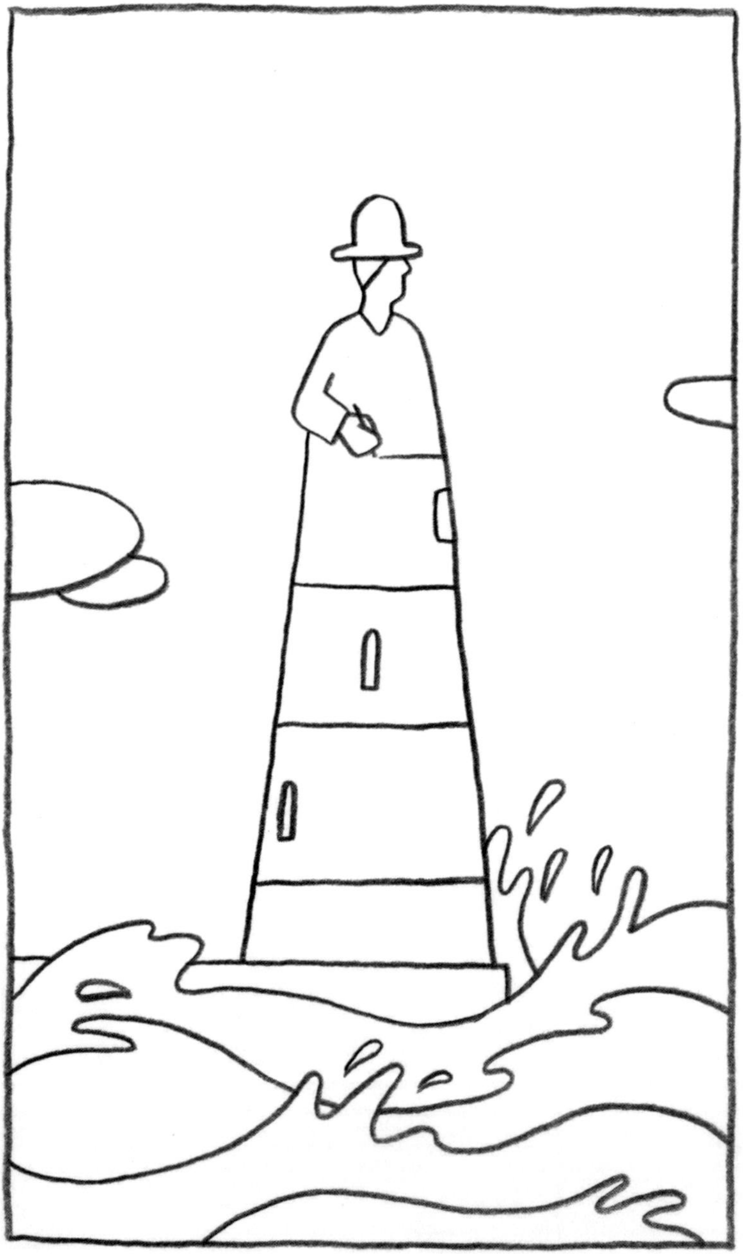

A STORY OF SELF-EMPOWERMENT
AND SEIZING CONTROL
OF ONE'S OWN NARRATIVE.

A STORY
OF RESILIENCE.

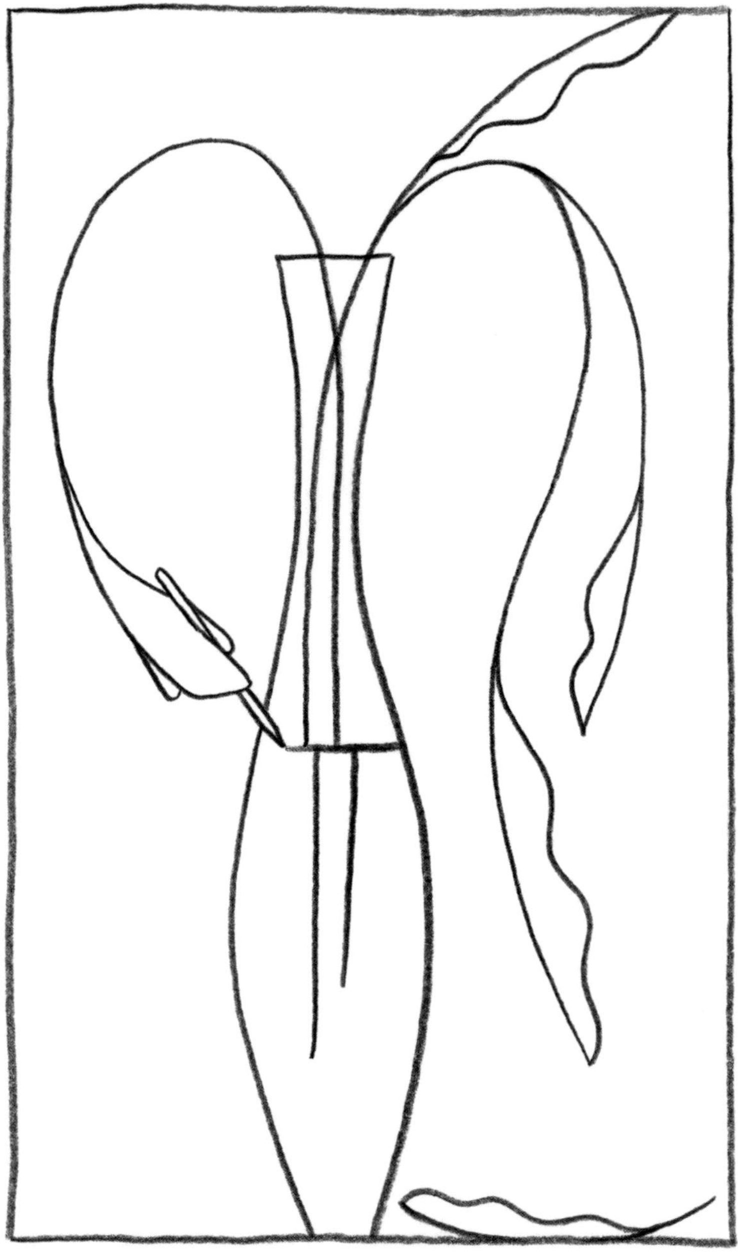

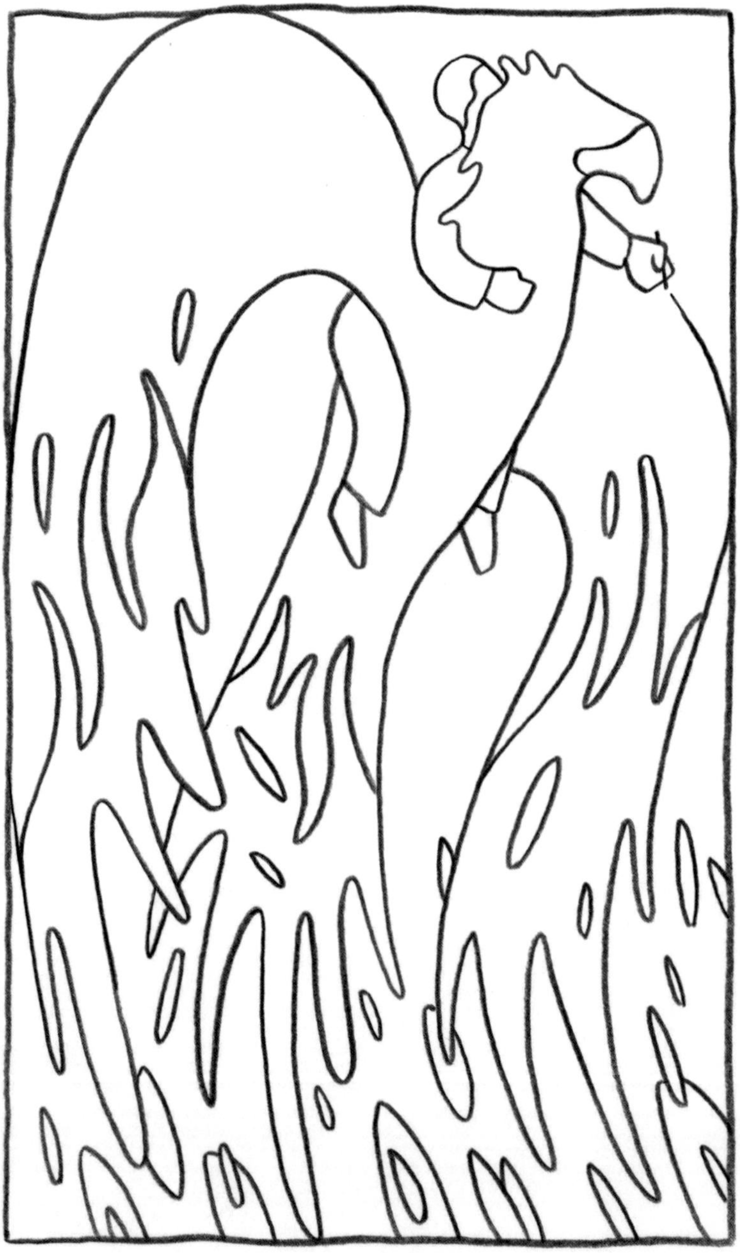

AND
HIDDEN STRENGTH.

MY ILLUSTRATIONS
OFTEN INCLUDE VISUAL METAPHORS AND SYMBOLS
TO HELP CONVEY ABSTRACT CONCEPTS, IDEAS,
OR EMOTIONS THAT MAY OTHERWISE REMAIN INVISIBLE.

WHAT IF,
THIS TIME,
I HAD MADE USE OF THEM UNKNOWINGLY?

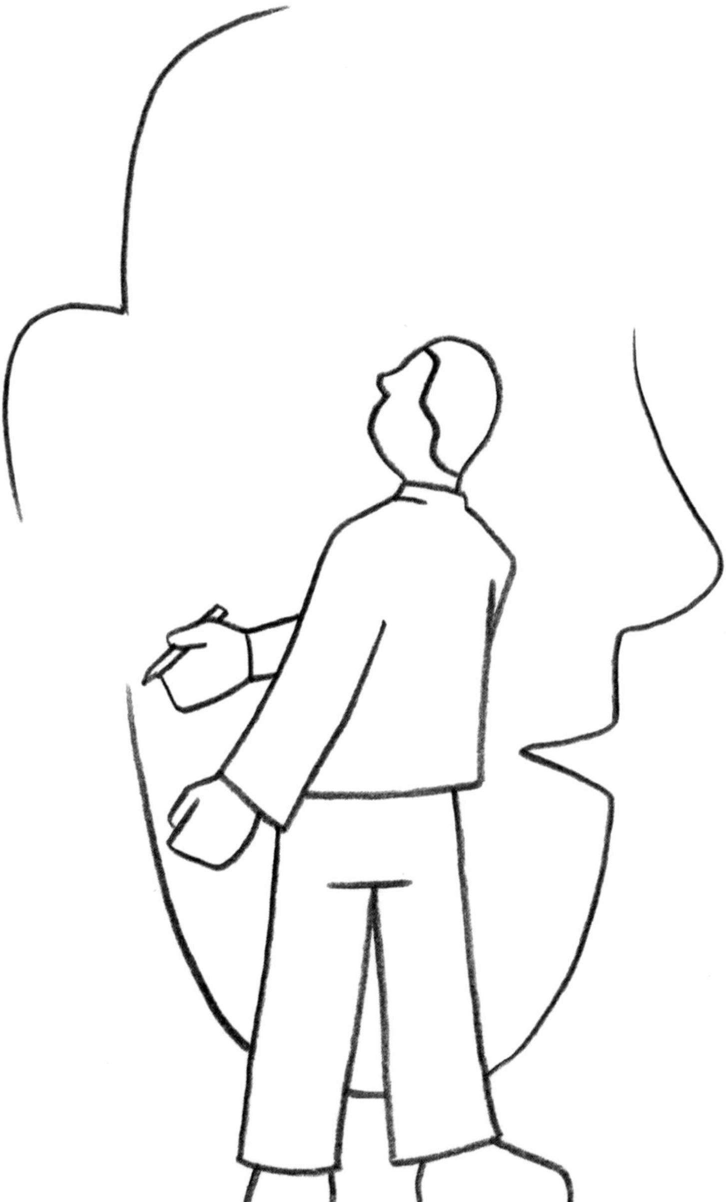

COULD THESE DRAWINGS
BE SELF-PORTRAITS
REVEALING A HIDDEN AND UNCONSCIOUS REALM OF
THOUGHTS AND FEELINGS?

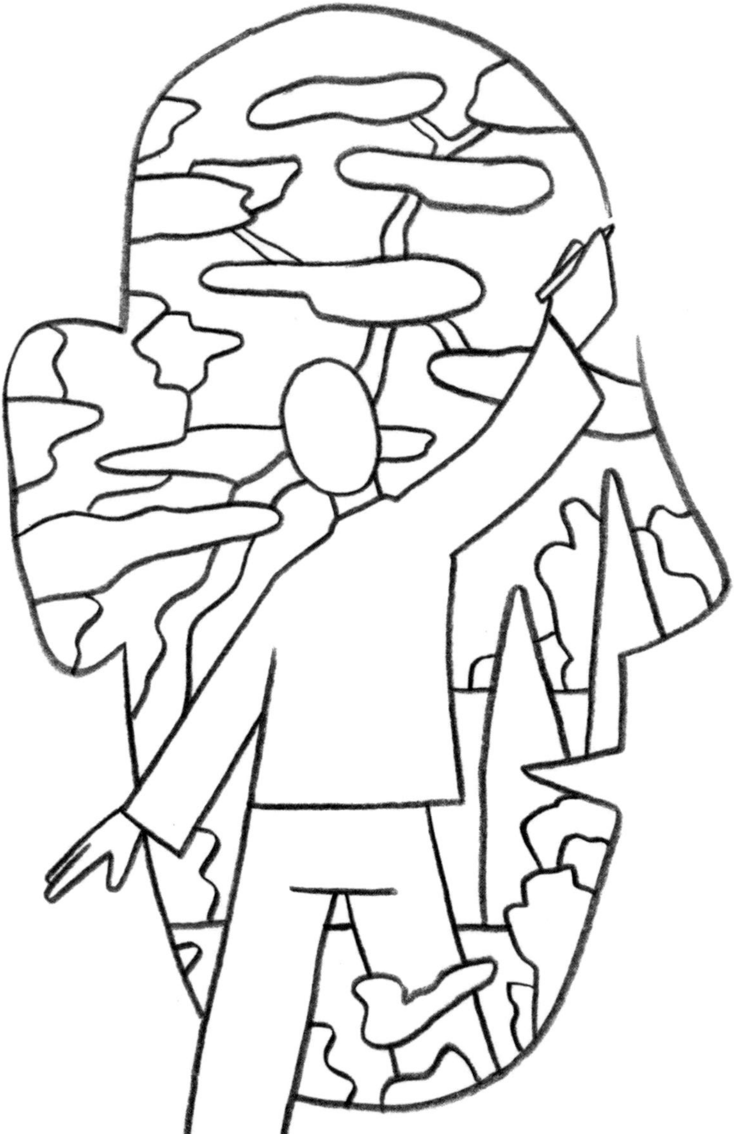

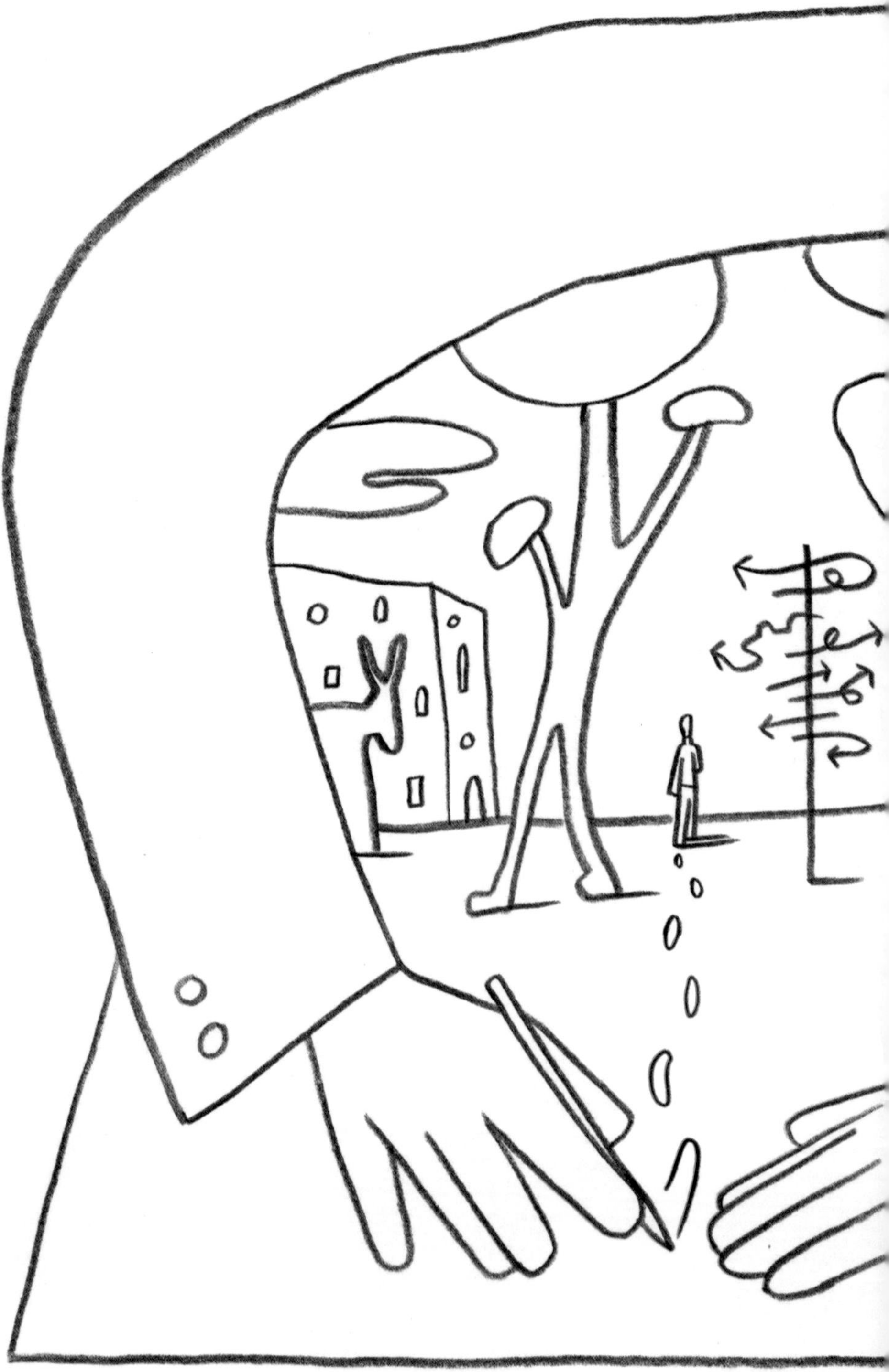

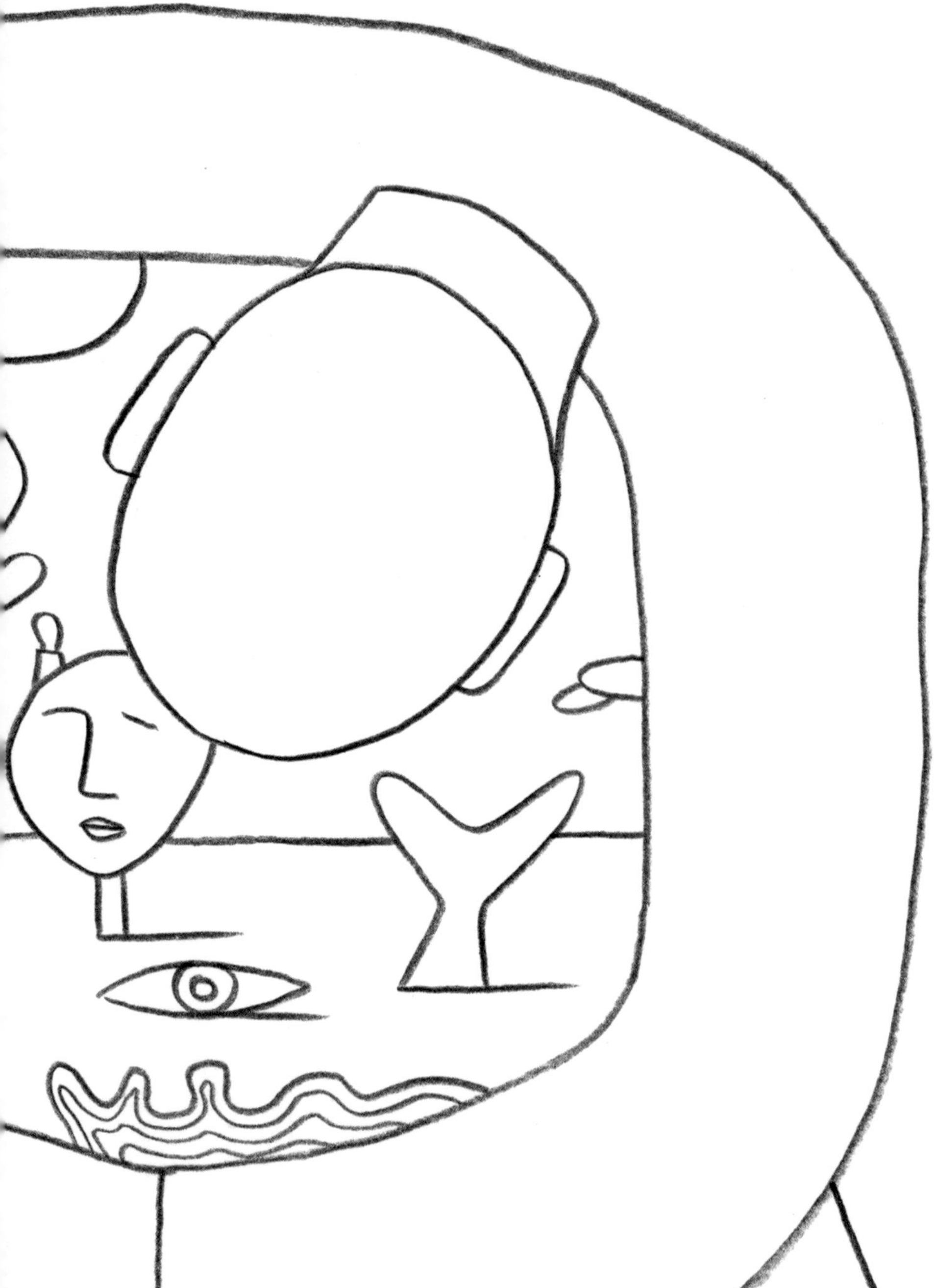

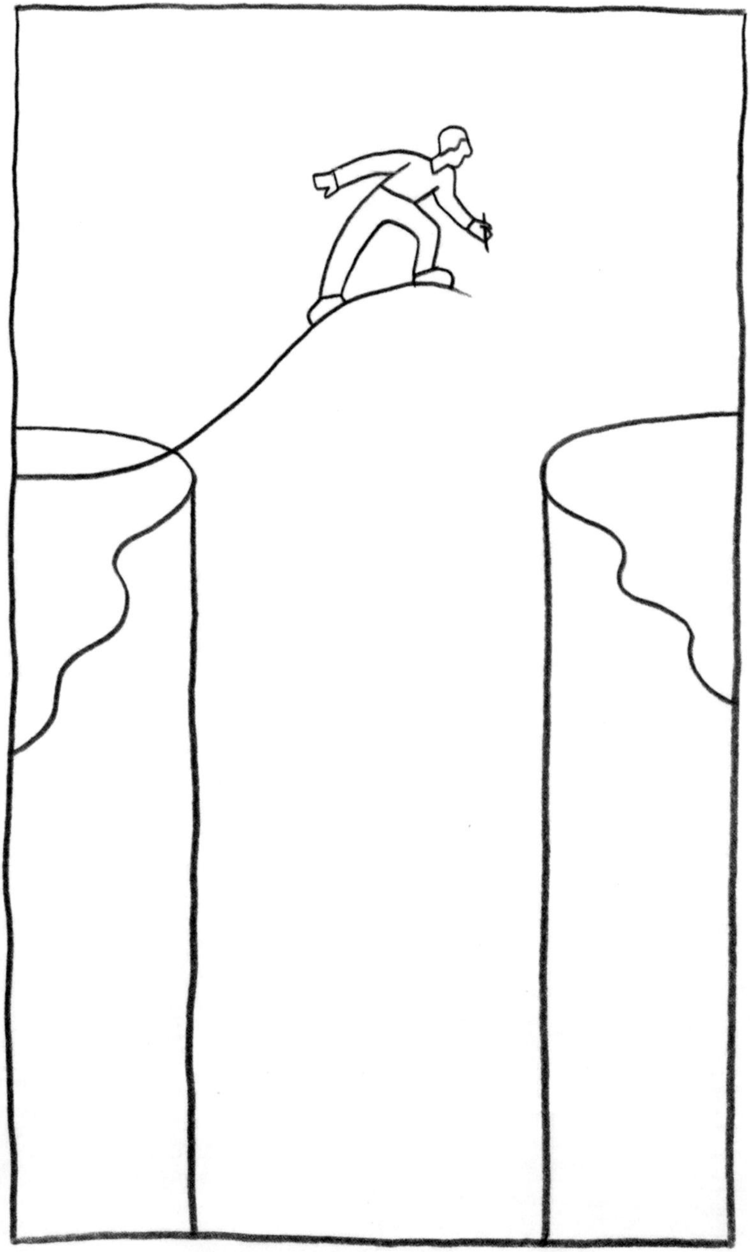

ARE THEY A VISUAL ANTITHESIS
TO MY BROTHER'S CONDITION,
CONTRASTING THE DEBILITATING DEPRESSION
I WAS TRYING TO MAKE SENSE OF?

PERHAPS THEY SYMBOLIZE
THE CURE-ALL
THAT I ALWAYS WISHED FOR
BUT HAVE DISAPPOINTINGLY LEARNED
DOES NOT EXIST?

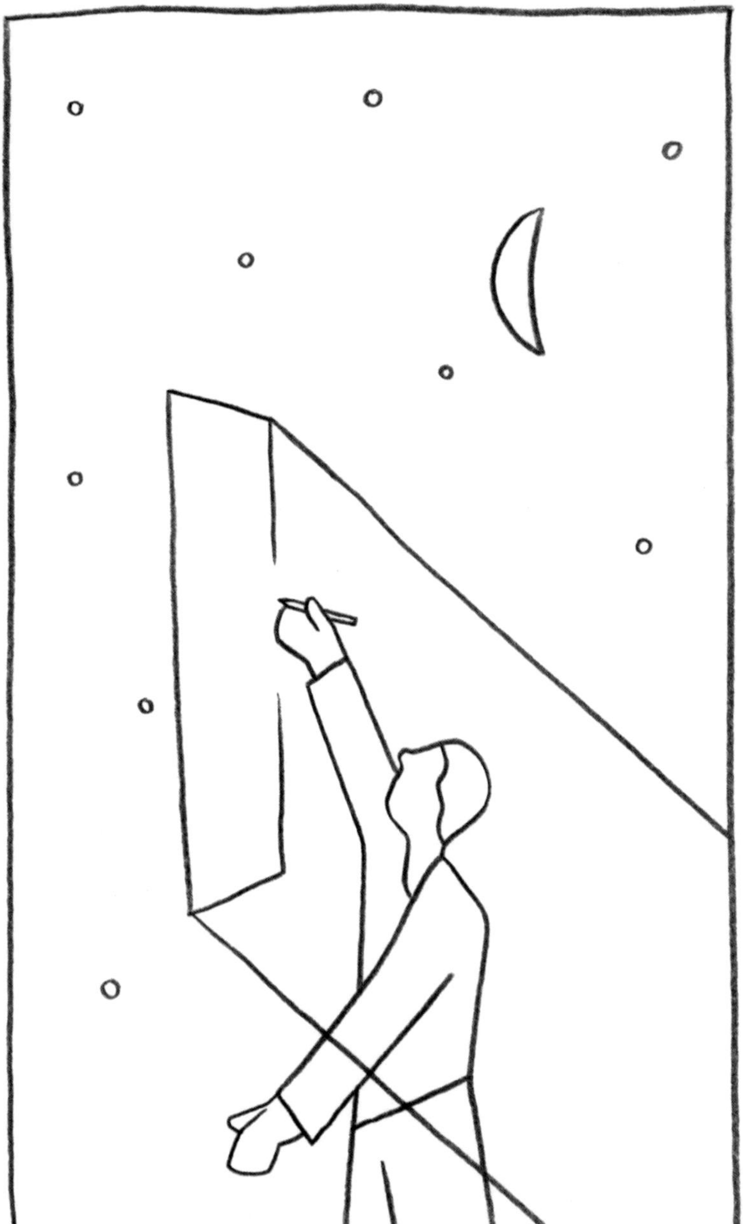

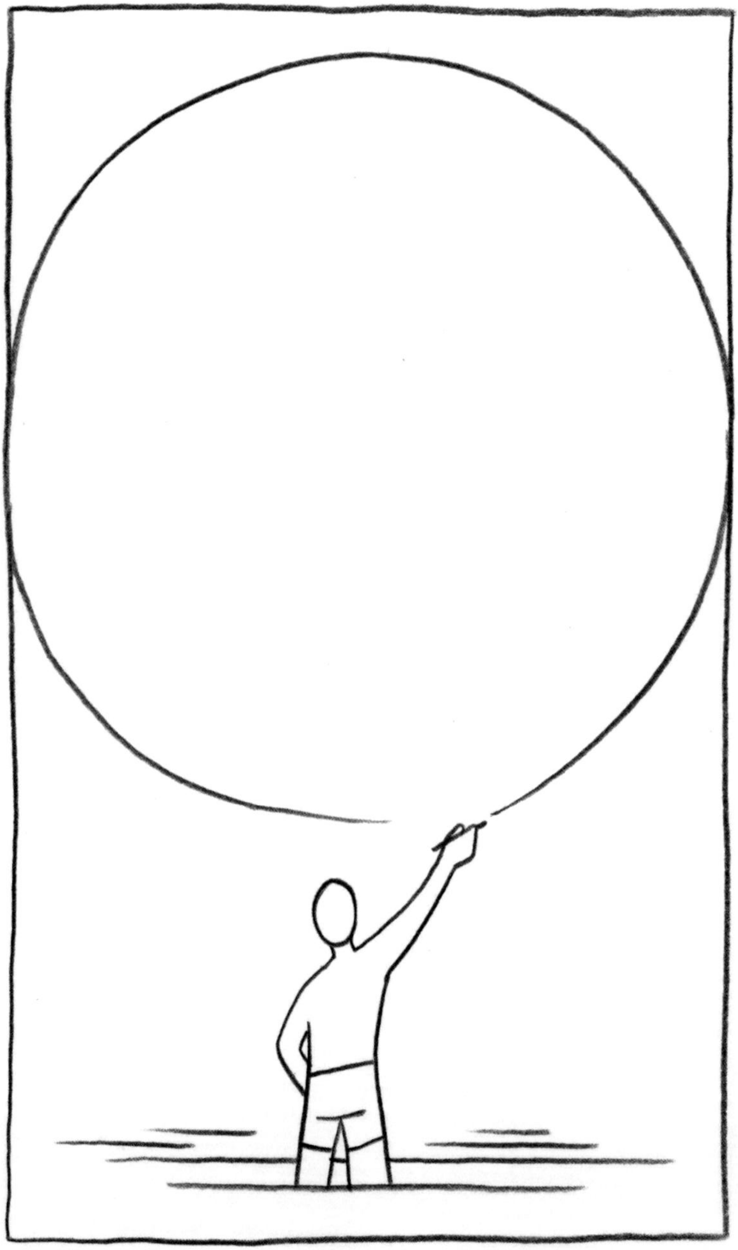

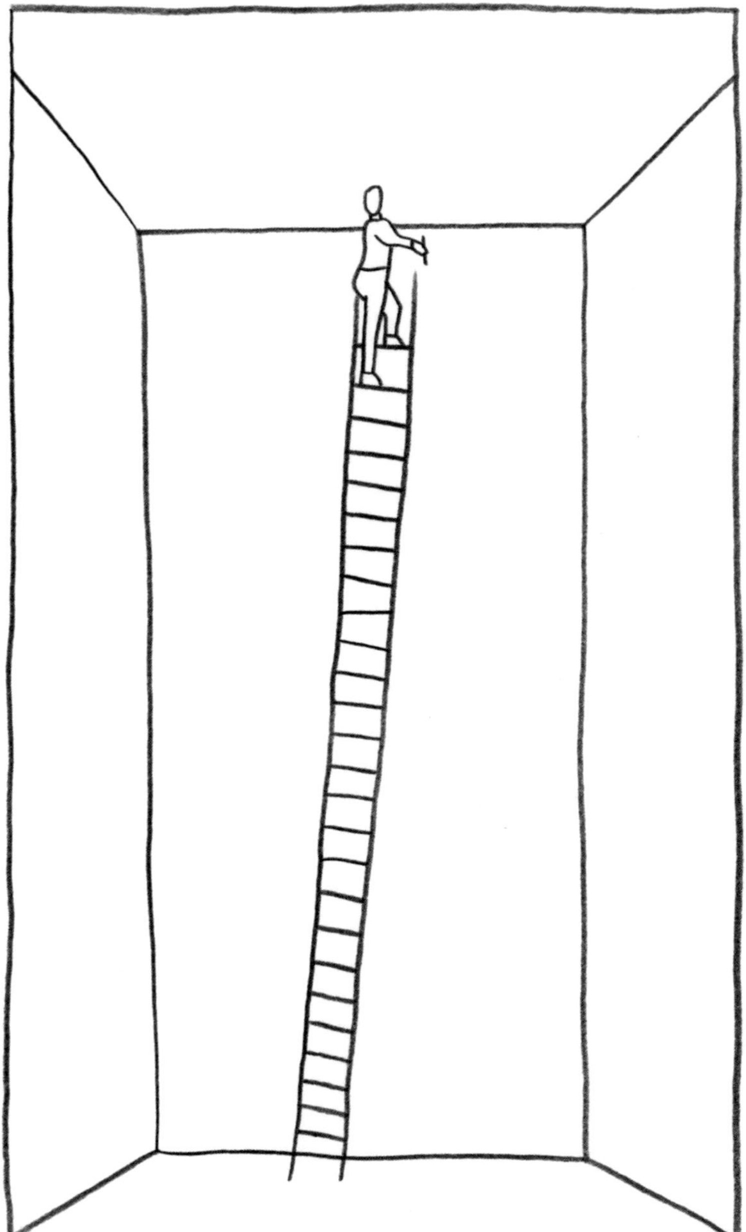

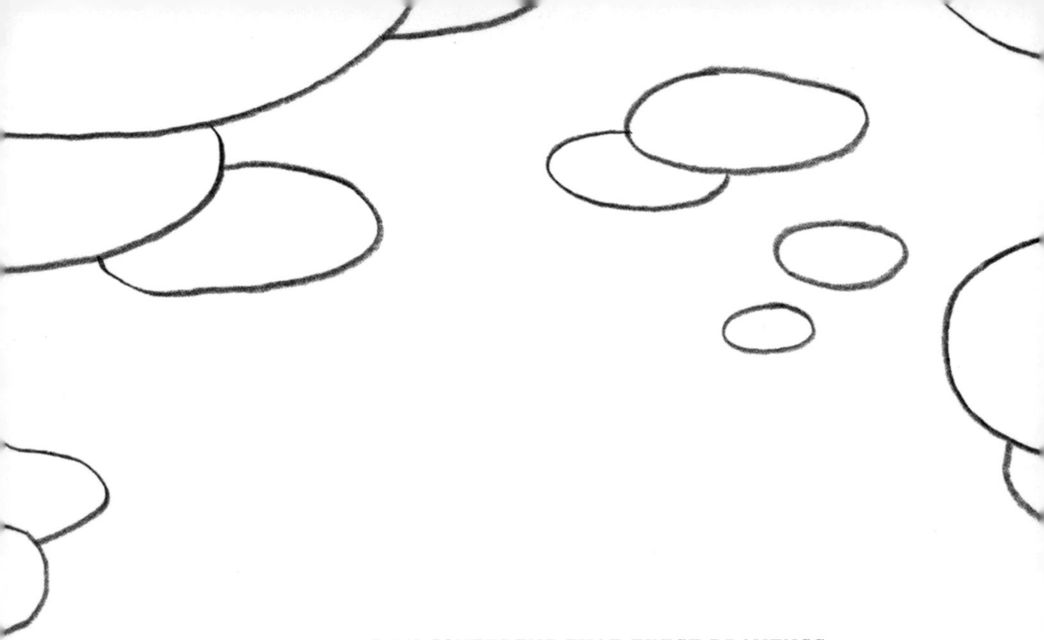

I AM CONFIDENT THAT THESE DRAWINGS HELPED ME VISUALIZE THE POSITIVE AND NAVIGATE THE STORMY TIDES OF THIS INSTRUCTIVE FAMILY JOURNEY THAT I EMBARKED ON THAT MORNING TEN YEARS AGO WHEN I ANSWERED MY MOM'S CALL.

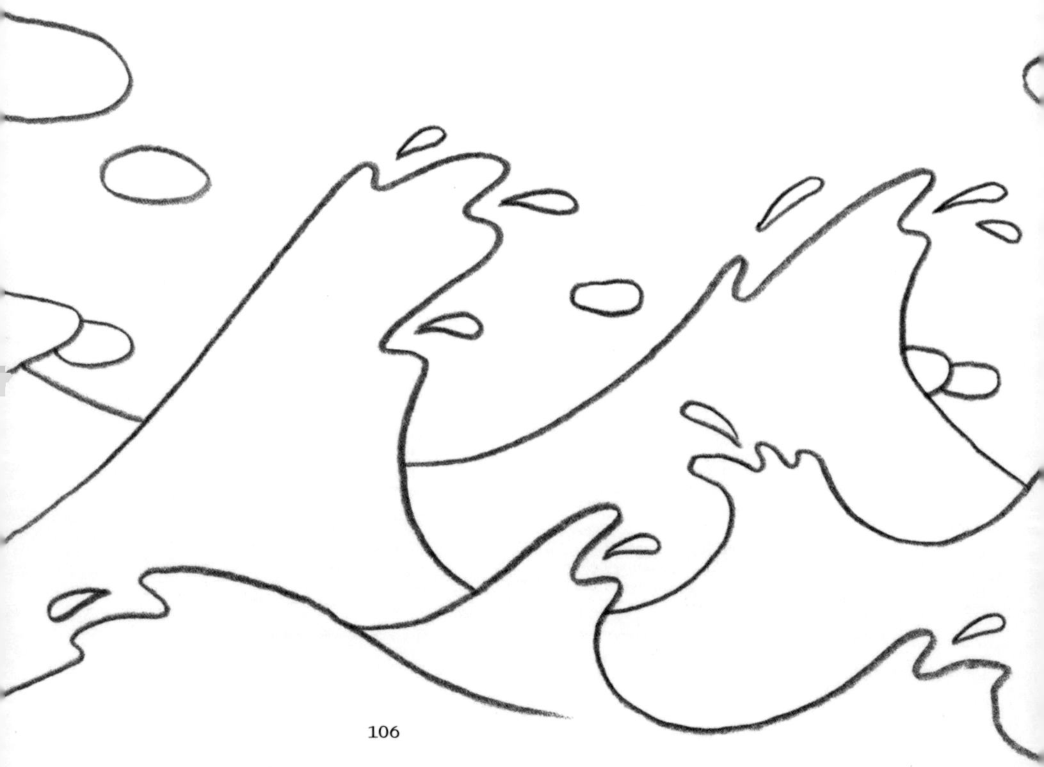

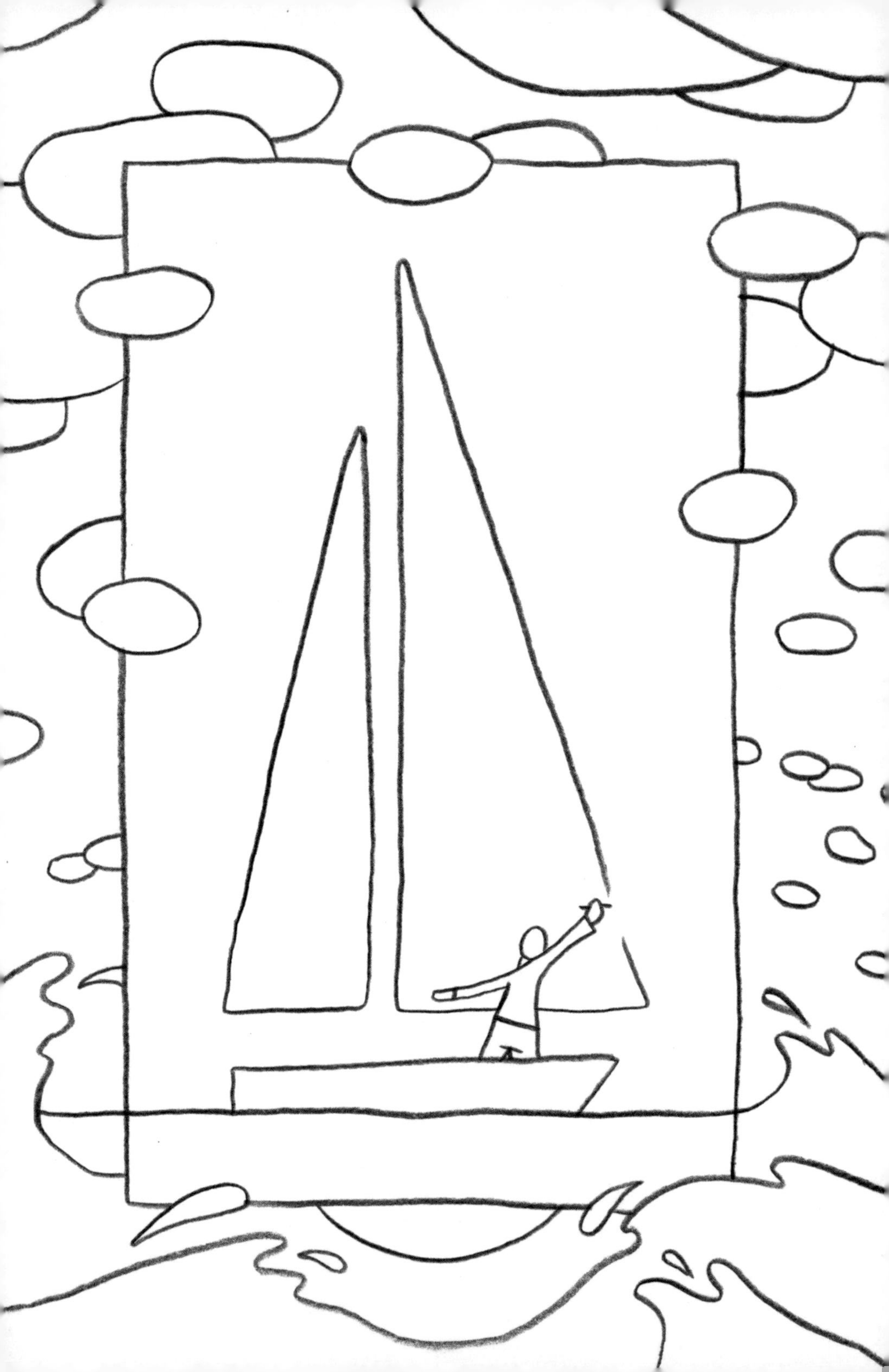

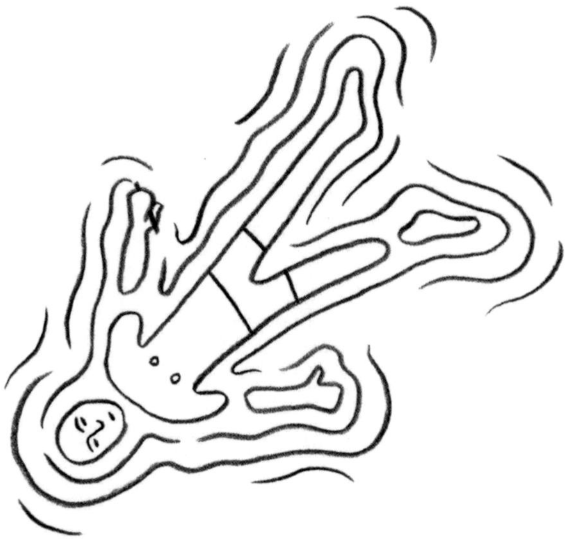

IF NOT A REMEDY TO MY BROTHER'S MENTAL ILLNESS OR AN EXPLANATION OF THE INEXPLICABLE, THEY BROUGHT ME A SENSE OF SERENITY TOWARDS AND ACCEPTANCE OF THIS SENSELESS TRAGEDY.

GRADUALLY, BETWEEN THE LINES
AND AMIDST A SEA OF FOG,
THINGS STARTED TAKING SHAPE.

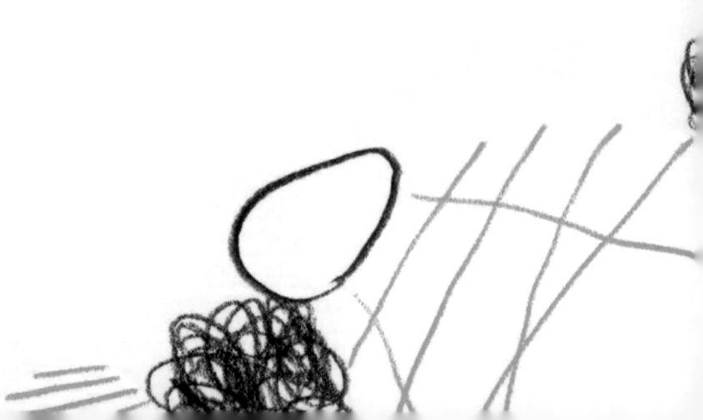

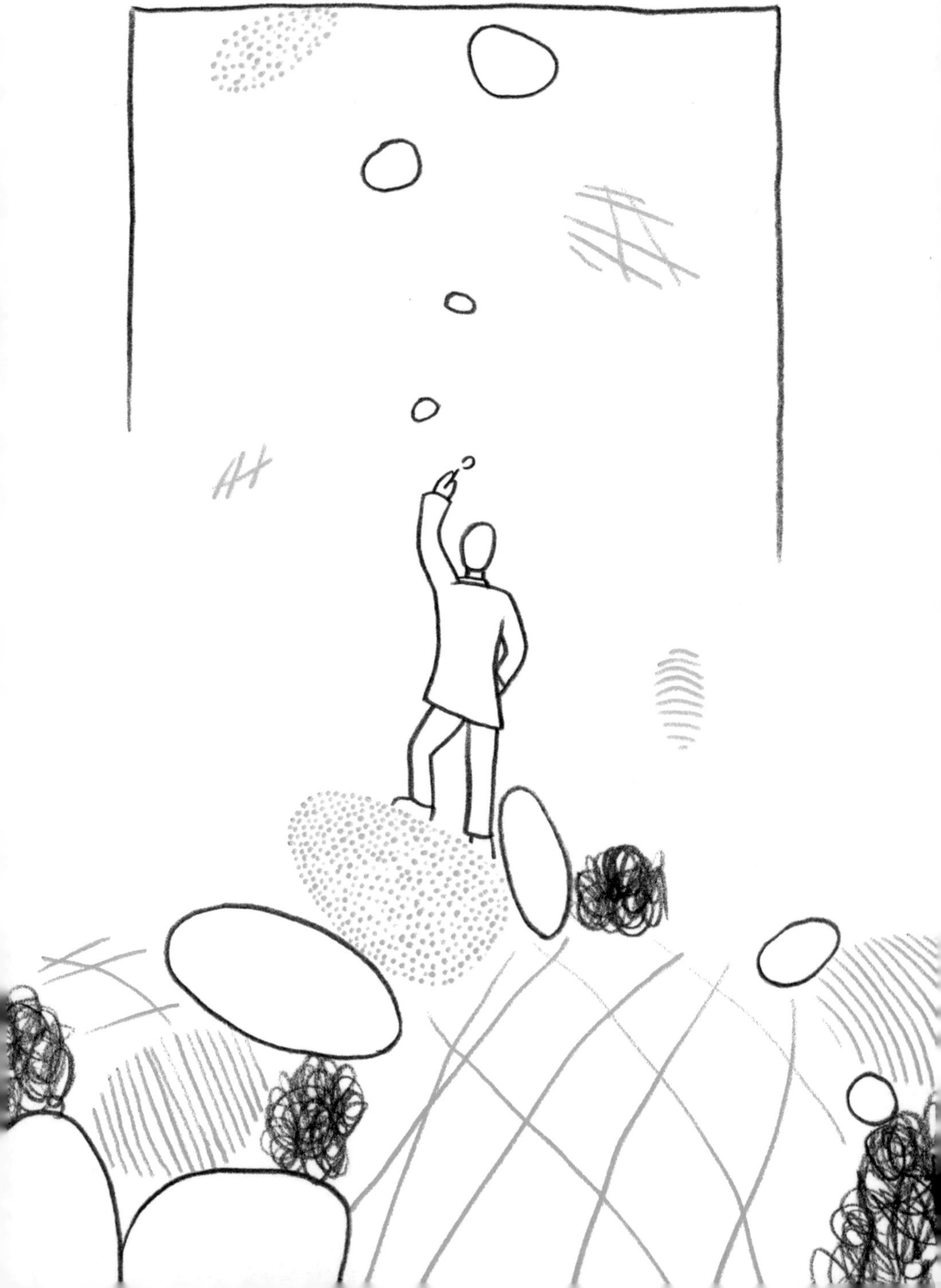

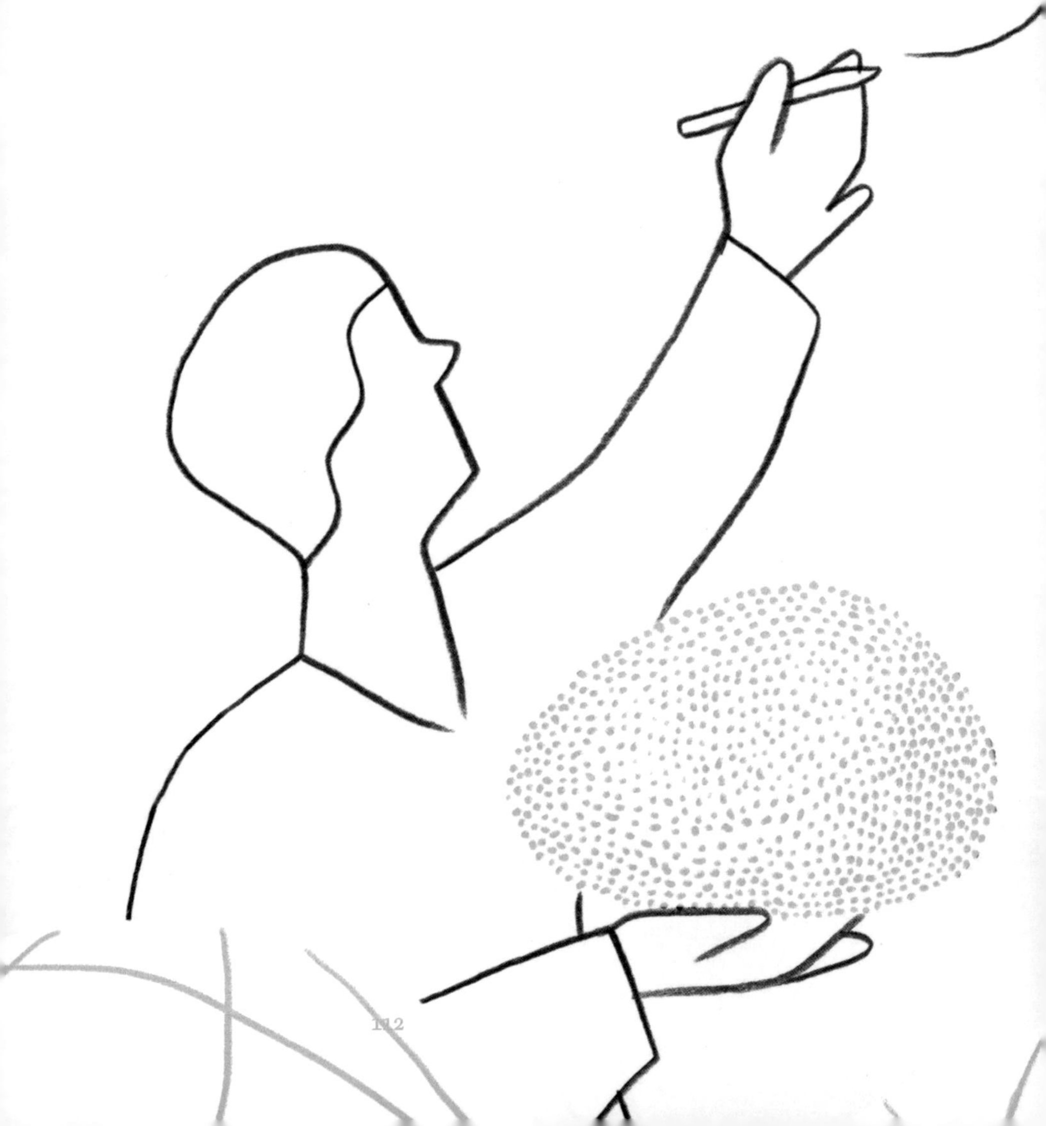

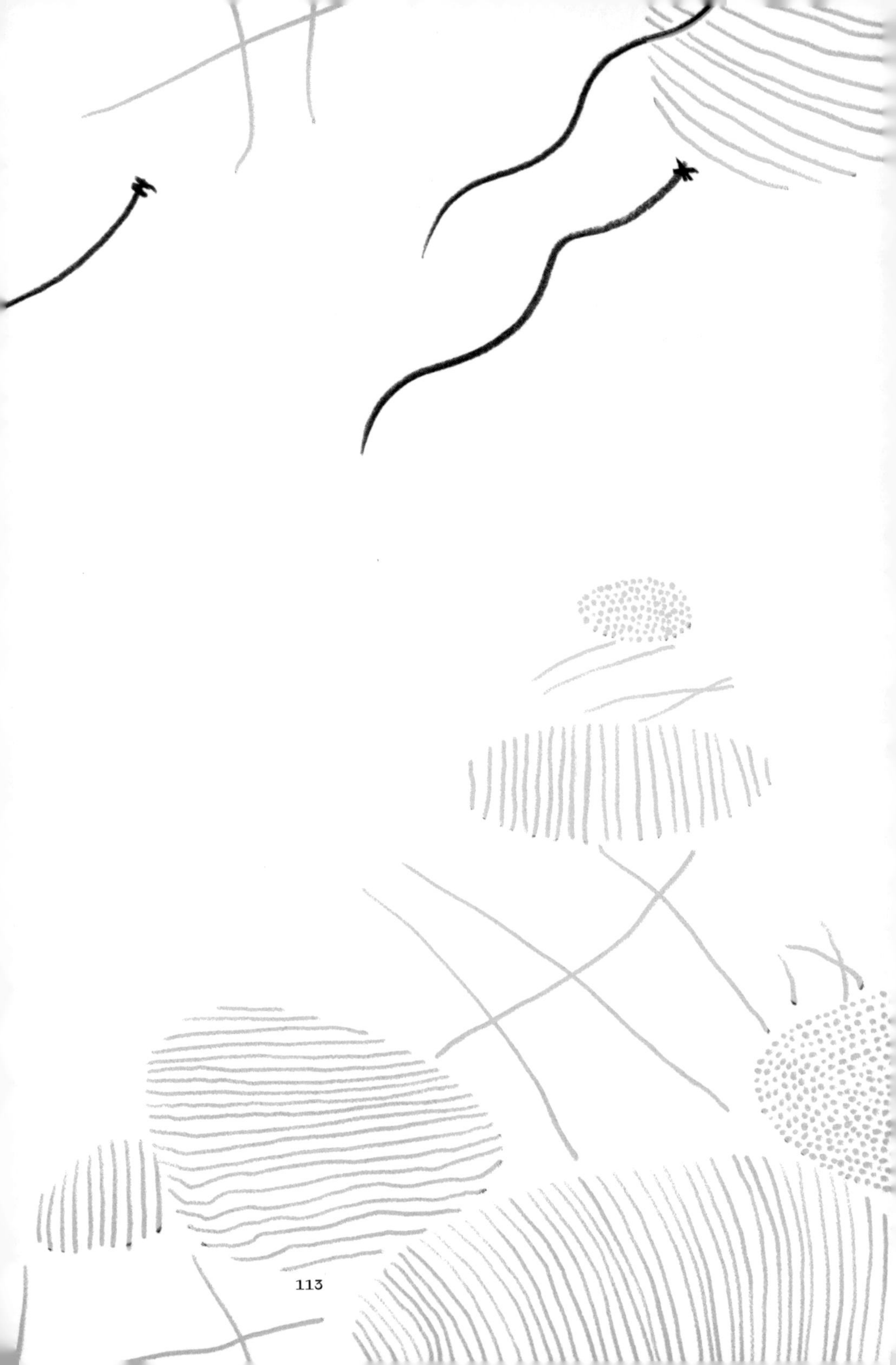

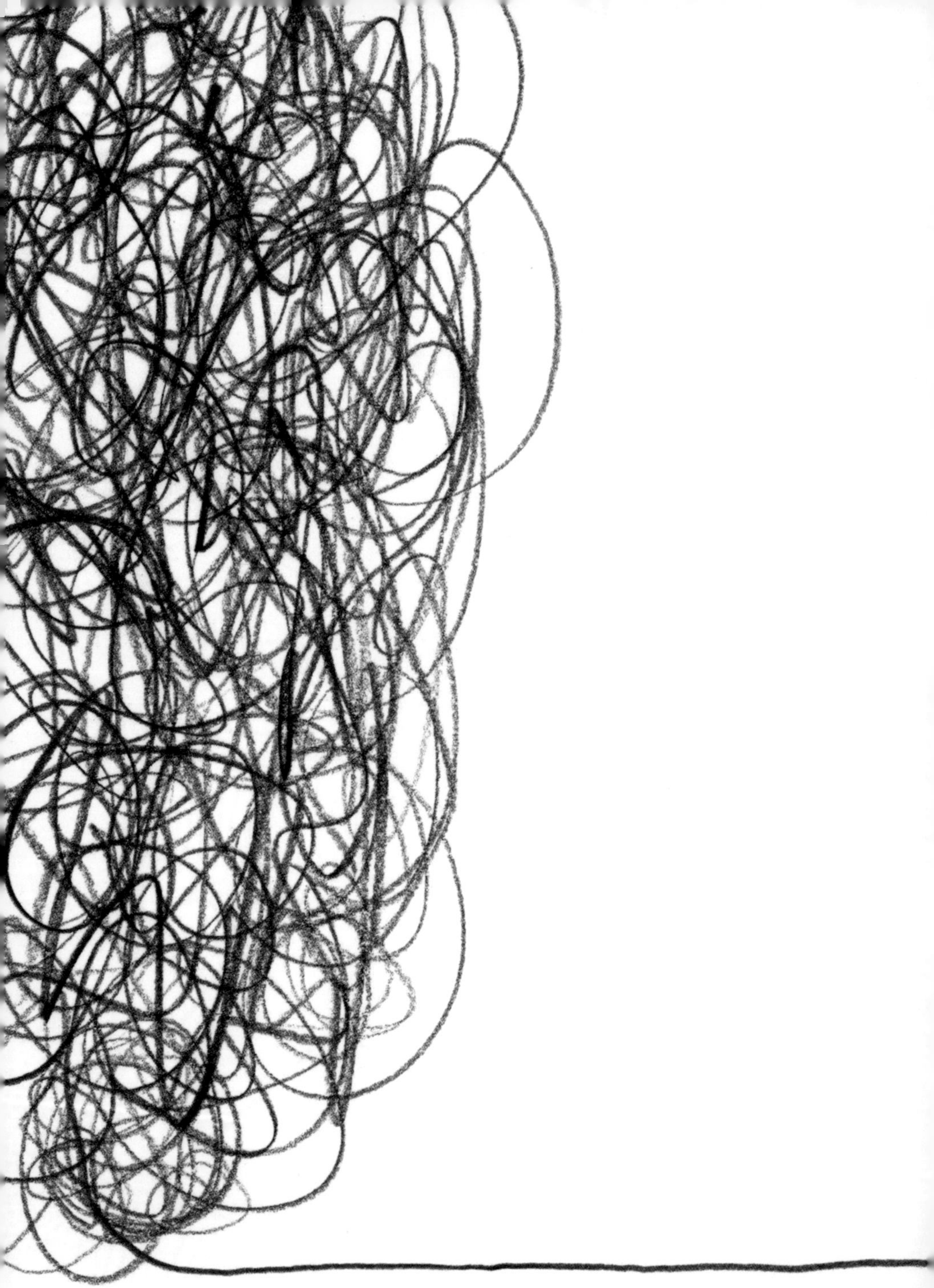

AND I FOUND
SOME RELIEF.

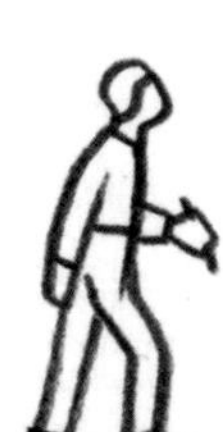

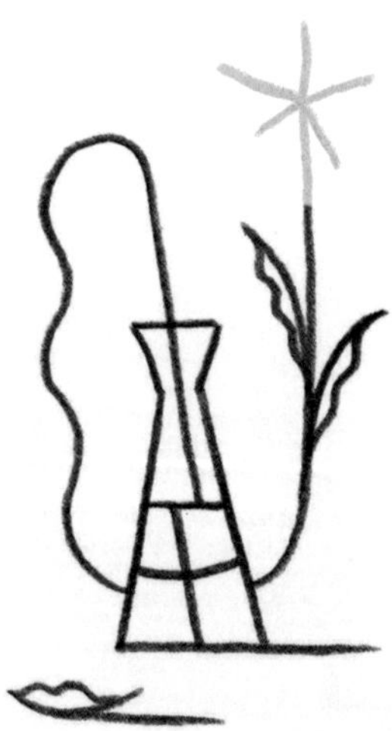

ADDENDUM

Most of the drawings published in this book originate from my sketchbooks and were created between 2013 and 2023. I redrew them to meet the requirements of this publication. Some of the original drawings were previously published in newspapers or magazines, including the cover image titled "Autofiction," which was featured on the cover of The Guardian's book review.

Living with a serious mental illness is incredibly challenging. It is also challenging to be close to someone who does. I have decided to share this journey and the struggles I encountered in the hope of providing some insight and understanding to those who have faced similar situations.

While I strongly believe that discovering one's personal outlet, as I did through drawing, can be valuable and self-empowering, I recognize that seeking professional assistance when needed is equally important. I hope these lines will contribute to a broader conversation about mental health and, eventually, help erase some of the stigma that remains attached to it.

ACKNOWLEDGMENTS

TO MY BROTHER, MOM, AND DAD.

Thank you, Sarah Bechter. And Christoph Abbrederis, Luna Al-Mousli, Marie Doerfler, Laura Edelbacher, Tobias Eichelberger, Stephan Göschl, Maria Kanzler, Philipp Leberle, Sebastian Leitinger, Oliver Riedel, and Erwin Schubert. Thank you, Elsa Kubik, Jana Lill, and Christian Schlager at EXEX, Ella Lupo at Purple Rain Illustrators, and everyone at Verlag für moderne Kunst, especially Anna Ebner and Silvia Jaklitsch.

ABOUT THE AUTHOR

FRANCESCO CICCOLELLA,
born in Salzburg in 1990, is an illustrator, graphic artist, and visual storyteller. His illustrations have graced the covers of international newspapers, magazines, and books. Renowned for his unique blend of wit and simplicity in form, he has earned prestigious recognition, including a Joseph Binder Award and a silver medal from the Society of Illustrators in New York. Since graduating from the University of Applied Arts Vienna, he has maintained a practice between commissioned and personal work, developing a distinctive visual voice of his own. He lives in Vienna, Austria.

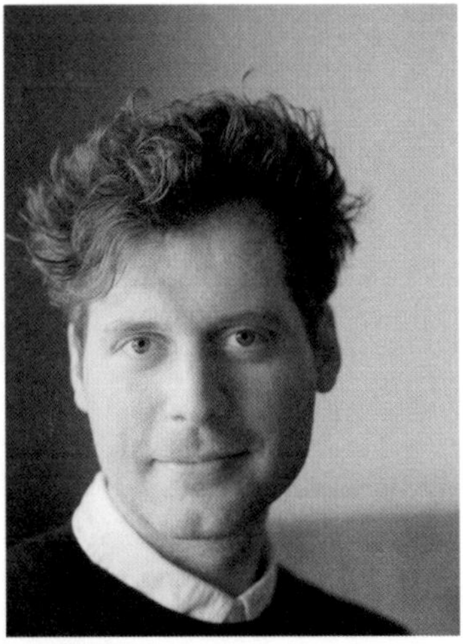

PORTRAIT by **Lisa Edi**

COLOPHON

DRAWINGS & TEXTS **Francesco Ciccolella**
mail@francescociccolella.com
francescociccolella.com

BOOK DESIGN **EXEX – Elsa Kubik, Christian Schlager, Jana Lill**
COPY EDITING **Rupert Hebblethwaite**
TYPEFACES **Qwerty** (by Ludovic Balland)
PAPER **Neobond, Arena Rough Natural, Arena Bulk Natural**
PRINTED IN AUSTRIA BY **Gerin Druck GmbH**

FIRST PUBLISHED IN 2023 BY
VfmK Verlag für moderne Kunst GmbH
Schwedenplatz 2/24
A-1010 Vienna
hello@vfmk.org
vfmk.org

ISBN 978-3-99153-049-7

DISTRIBUTION
EUROPE **LKG**, lkg-va.de
UK **Cornerhouse Publications**, cornerhousepublications.org
USA **D.A.P.**, artbook.com

BIBLIOGRAPHIC INFORMATION PUBLISHED BY
the Deutsche Nationalbibliothek
The Deutsche Nationalbibliothek lists this publication
in the Deutsche Nationalbibliografie;
detailed bibliographic data is available at dnb.de

If you are having thoughts of suicide,
or are concerned that someone you know may be,
international helplines can be found at suicidestop.com

KINDLY SUPPORTED BY

STADT : SALZBURG

Federal Ministry
Republic of Austria
Arts, Culture,
Civil Service and Sport